CANADIAN MEDICAL LIVES

SIR CHARLES TUPPER

Fighting Doctor to Father of Confederation

Jock Murray O.C. and Janet Murray

Series Editor: T.P. Morley, M.D.

Associated Medical Services, Incorporated
and
Fitzhenry & Whiteside

Fitzhenry & Whiteside
195 Allstate Parkway
Markham, Ontario L3R 4T8

Book Design: Darrell McCalla

Printing and Binding: University of Toronto Press Incorporated

Fitzhenry & Whiteside wishes to acknowledge the generous assistance
and ongoing support of The Book Publishing Industry Development
Programme of the Department of Communications, The Canada Council,
and The Ontario Arts Council.

Care has been taken to trace the ownership of copyright material used
in the text, including the illustrations. The author and publisher welcome
any information enabling them to rectify any reference or credit in
subsequent editions.

Canadian Cataloguing in Publication Data

Murray, Jock, 1938-
  Sir Charles Tupper: fighting doctor to Father of Confederation

(Canadian medical lives)
Includes index

ISBN 1-55041-183-7

1. Tupper, Charles, Sir, 1821-1915. 2. Prime ministers – Canada –
Biography. 3. Prime ministers – Nova Scotia – Biography. 4 Canada –
Politics and government – 1867-1896.* 5. Nova Scotia – Politics and
government – 19th century.* 6. Physicians – Canada – Biography.
I. Murray, Janet, 1937- . II. Title. III. Series.

FC526.T8M87 1998   971.05'5'092   C98-931313-1
F1033.T8M87 1998

Sir Charles Tupper.

We dedicate this chronicle of our country's past
to our grandchildren
Samuel and Celia Murray Wandio
and Carson and Madison Murray
who are our country's future

CANADIAN MEDICAL LIVES SERIES

The story of the Hannah Institute for the History of Medicine has been told by John B. Neilson and G.R. Paterson in *Associated Medical Services Incorporated: A History (1987)*. Dr. Donald R. Wilson, then President of AMS, and the Board of directors decided that the Institute should produce a series of biographies as one of its undertakings.

This is the twenty-third volume in the series. All these biographies can be obtained through the retail book trade or from Fitzhenry & Whiteside, 195 Allstate Parkway, Markham ON L3R 4T8.

When Charles Tupper, a young Nova Scotian country doctor, discovered the power of his oratory at a local political meeting, his career and the future of Nova Scotia and Canada were changed forever. He was admired and reviled but he never surrendered to his opponents once he had started out on a reforming crusade. Between periods of great political activity he returned to the practice of medicine and to his loyal and devoted patients. He saw the need for a major university and medical school in the maritime provinces, for a national medical organization (he was elected the first President of the Canadian Medical Association), for maritime union and equality among the colonies within the Empire, for a railroad from sea to sea and for a union of all the regions with the confederation of Canada. History has not always given him his due.

There is no shortage of meritorious subjects. Willing and capable authors are harder to acquire. AMS is therefore deeply grateful to authors who have committed their time and skill to the series.

T.P. Morley
Series Editor
1999

CANADIAN MEDICAL LIVES SERIES

Duncan Graham by Robert B. Kerr & Douglas Waugh

Bill Mustard by Marilyn Dunlop

Joe Doupe by Terence Moore

Emily Stowe by Mary Beacock Fryer

Clarence Hincks by Charles G. Roland

Francis A.C. Scrimger, V.C., by Suzanne Kingsmill

Earle P. Scarlett by F.W. Musselwhite

R.G. Ferguson by Stuart Houston

Harold Griffith by Richard Bodman & Dierdre Gillies

Maude Abbott by Douglas Waugh

William Boyd by Ian Carr

J.C. Boileau Grant by C.L.N. Robinson

R.M. Bucke by Peter A. Rechnitzer

William Henry Drummond by J.B. Lyons

Alan Brown by A.B. Kingsmill

Harold N. Segall by C.G. Roland

William R. Beaumont by Julian A. Smith

David M. Baltzan by Verne Clemence

Jean I. Gunn by Natalie Riegler

Leonard Albert Miller by John R. Martin

Anderson Ruffin Abbott by M. Dalyce Newby

Brock Chisholm by Allan Irving

Sir Charles Tupper by Jock Murray O.C. and Janet Murray

CONTENTS

Introduction   11

Chapter 1   Early Years   13

Chapter 2   Edinburgh   23

Chapter 3   Country Doctor   35

Chapter 4   Political Life Begins   41

Chapter 5   Maritime Union   46

Chapter 6   Confederation   63

Chapter 7   Senior Physician and Politician   74

Chapter 8   A Trace of Albumin   95

Chapter 9   On Guard for Thee   107

Chapter 10   Envoi   118

Chapter 11   Epilogue   125

Appendices   A Genealogy and Chronology   132

               Obituary of Sir Charles Tupper
               by Sir William Osler   143

               Bibliography   145

               Index   151

Acknowledgements

W e are grateful to all those who gave us so much help over the last four years as we sought information on Tupper in Halifax, Edinburgh, Ottawa, Amherst and London.

Before acknowledging the individuals who made our task easier, we would like to generally recognize the staff of the Provincial Archives of Nova Scotia, the National Library of Canada, the National Archives of Canada, The Wellcome Institute of London, the library of the Royal College of Physicians of London, the Cumberland County Museum (Nova Scotia), the Archives of the Canadian Medical Association, the Bexley Museum, the Public Record Office of London, Edinburgh University Library, the Archives of the Royal Infirmary and Lothian Region Health Board in Edinburgh, the Kellogg Library of Dalhousie Medical School, the Audio-Visual Department of Dalhousie University Medical School. Their efficient, kind and knowledgeable assistance each time we arrived at their desks with yet another request, we remember with gratitude.

We also thank Dr. Michael Barfoot, Dr. Ian Cameron, Jo Currie, Allan C. Dunlop, Donald MacLean, Dr. Allan Marble, Dr. Phillip Hartling, Dr. Alan J. MacLeod, Dr. James Darragh, Owen McInerney, Helen Hatcher, Roxy Pelham, Suellen Murray and Bruce Murray. A special thank you to Mr. Albert Fowler of Bexleyheath, Kent, England, who invited two strangers from Canada into his home to show them the garden house from Tupper's Bexleyheath home, and who shared his considerable knowledge of the area.

While grateful for their assistance and advice, we accept all responsibility for error or omission.

Introduction

This is the biography of a physician, a country doctor in Nova Scotia, trained at Edinburgh, in the expectation that he would return to his home town and spend his life in the practice of medicine. And that is what he did for thirteen years, with no thought that there was more from life than his family in Amherst and the full practice of his skills in the service of his patients.

Thirteen years later a minor event at a local political meeting put him briefly on the stage to introduce a politician. This lit a spark, evident to others in his remarks, and his career and the future of Nova Scotia and Canada was changed forever.

Dramatic, you say? Well, the life and times of Charles Tupper were tumultuous, interwoven with the dramatic beginnings of our country and the volatile and colourful politics of that age.

He was admired and reviled.

He was regarded as the visionary and principled man who saw the importance of free education for all children, of statistics as a tool for improved health care, of better care of the poor, of better hospital care in the community, of public health; he saw the need for a major university unfettered by religion, for a medical school for the maritime region, for a national medical organization, for an equality among the colonies within the Empire, for maritime union and later for union of all the regions into the confederation of Canada, and the binding of the country by a railroad from sea to sea. He did much to see all this accomplished.

On the other hand he could be seen as a powerful man striding into a room determined to accomplish his ends, no notes in hand, with a face like a storm cloud; a no-nonsense, humourless, demanding, dominating manner that swept away any niceties of discussion that had gone before. He seldom lost an argument and seldom lost a cause. But in his wake he left a bewildered, bruised and often resentful group more used to a subtle and serpentine political process. In debate he was clever, logical, aggressive and ruthless, pummelling his opponents into submission long after the point was won. His brilliance was acknowledged but even his admirers, and there were many, recognized that his lack of finesse and the absence of a gentle hand in his pursuit of causes sometimes limited his effectiveness and acceptability.

Physicians will not necessarily admire the style of the sterotypical physician-surgeons of that day, with their pragmatic and powerful approach to every issue; opinionated, but willing and happy to stand by their personal opinions in the interest of their patients, a confidence based on their training and experience, and on their awareness of their position in the community. When Dr. Charles Tupper, general physician and surgeon, was pushed onto the political stage he embraced it fully, but with the style and approach of a physician. Politicians of the day and historians of the era often saw Tupper's unique style unfavourably, being more used to the style of lawyer-politicians, who seemed to play at debate and politics. To Tupper, it was never a game.

Tupper was an excellent physician and surgeon. After he became a politician his patients were his province and his country. The approach bewildered his friends and his enemies, but he succeeded where others had failed.

CHAPTER 1

Early Years

The young man on the deck of the brigantine Huntington sailing out of Windsor, Nova Scotia, in the spring of 1840 was "of medium height, straight, muscular and wiry, and with intense nervous energy, which gave him quickness of movement and ceaseless mental activity."[1] His name was Charles Tupper. He was 19 years old and he was on his way to Edinburgh University to study medicine at one of the outstanding medical schools of the world. Although he could not have known it then, he was making the first of forty transatlantic crossings. More important for him and for his country, he was embarking on a life which would bring him not only distinction in medicine, but also an illustrious career as a politician, statesman and nation builder.

Charles was born in East Amherst, a small community near the village of Amherst, Nova Scotia, on 2 July 1821.[2] Amherst was a small township in Cumberland County near the Isthmus of Chignecto, which connected the British colonies of Nova Scotia and New Brunswick. It had been projected as a township in 1759, although there had been a French Acadian settlement in the area as early as 1672. It was named in honour of Lord Jeffrey Amherst (1717-1797), the English general who, along with Admiral Boscawen, had captured the French fortress of Louisbourg in Isle Royale (now Cape Breton) in 1758.

Charles's father, the Reverend Charles Tupper, D.D., and his wife, the former Miriam (Lockhart) Low of Parrsboro[3] had moved to a twelve acre farm in East Amherst from a previous posting in the Nova Scotia village of River Philip. He had been pastor for the Baptist congregation there but, as early as 1819, had spent part of his time at the First Baptist Church in Amherst. He moved his family to East Amherst in 1821 shortly before Charles was born.

After a short stay in Amherst the family moved again, this time to Saint John, New Brunswick, where Rev. Tupper became pastor of the Baptist Church. There were further moves, to Bedeque, Prince Edward Island, and Fredericton, New Brunswick, but each time the family returned to Amherst. In addition to his work as a Baptist minister, Rev. Tupper, who was a self-educated man with a reading knowledge of thirteen languages, was principal of a grammar school in Amherst and later of a Baptist seminary in Fredericton.[4]

The Tupper home was an intellectually stimulating one. Rev. Charles Tupper was said to be "a diligent and systematic pastor, a clear, vigorous writer, and an earnest and able preacher . . . for many years he was one of the most prominent ministers of any denomination in Nova Scotia."[5] He had a large library considering the time and place. He had become a schoolmaster at the age of nineteen, and was ordained a Baptist minister when he was twenty-five. He was widely recognized for his learning and had read the Bible in English, Greek, Latin, Hebrew, French, Syriac, German and Italian, and the New Testament in Spanish and Portuguese. Clearly he would be a strong teacher for his children, and much of Charles's early education was at the stern direction of his father. Stern he was, rigid in his moral beliefs, unbending in his principles and strong in their advocacy. He didn't shrink from controversy or challenge, and one of his earliest writings was a book on baptism addressed to the Reverend I.W.D. Gray who held opposite views, and he later engaged in a baptismal skirmish with the Reverend Trotter of Antigonish. Despite great antagonism in the community he formed the colony's first Temperance Society in Annapolis, with 20 members, on 31 December 1819. Many of his personality traits were passed along to his son. But, unlike his son, he was not a captivating orator and it was noted, even in his obituary, that he was full of knowledge but dull.[6] The Reverend Charles was a simple man, with no debts during his life, and at his death it was noted that no debts were passed on to his children. He "wore a plain coat, but it was paid for." He was said to be a balanced man, true to the moral code he preached, "cautious and enterprising, merciful and just, firm in his belief yet courteous to those that differed from him. He was generous and was one of the first in the province to offer support to foreign missionaries. There was no egotism in his piety or plainness, and later in life when he was asked about the prominence of his children and the knighthood to his son Charles, said, "I am like the lady who, when informed that her son had been promoted, said, 'My good friends, I feel neither better or worse.'" For his contributions to his flock and his community he was awarded an honorary Doctor of Divinity by Acadia University.

Visitors to the Tupper home included James William Johnstone, leader of the Conservative Party. Years later, when they met in a different forum, Charles Tupper remembered that as a child he had gathered raspberries in the field and brought them to Johnstone who was a visiting at this time. The Rev. Tupper's associate pastor in the Amherst Baptist Church was the Rev. Samuel McCully, whose son, the Hon. Jonathon McCully, became a Judge of the Supreme Court and a Father of Confederation.

The Tuppers were descended from Eliakim Tupper of Lebanon, Connecticut, who was one of a group of New England planters who had immigrated to Nova Scotia at the invitation of the Nova Scotia governor, to take over the farmlands in the Annapolis Valley, farmlands which had been confiscated from the French-speaking Acadians in 1755.[7] Eliakim was descended from Thomas Tupper who emigrated to Sandwich, Massachusetts, from England in 1621, finally remaining in New England in 1631 after two trips back to England.

The Tupper family had come originally from Germany , where the name had evolved from "Toppfern". The family was strongly Protestant and with a tradition that one of the early members of the family had been a collaborator of Martin Luther.[8] The name "Martin" appears frequently in the family tree, which includes the English Victorian poet, Martin Tupper. Many ministers of the church have their place in the tree, including missionaries to both native Americans and native Canadians, sea captains, magistrates, selectmen and landowners.

Miriam Lockhart Low[9] was a young widow with six children when she married the Reverend Charles Tupper. Writing about her in the Christian Messenger many years later, her husband said that she was a slender and delicate woman who was never very strong physically, and was modest and diffident in her manner. Her shyness was a problem when she first attended school. She recoiled from the harshness of the teachers and seemed to do poorly. Her father recognizing the problem, took her out of the school until the teachers were willing to change their attitude towards her. When they finally agreed, Miriam returned to school, and under a different regime blossomed into an excellent student.

She had been married young to John Low of Westmorland, New Brunswick; and they moved to Castine, Maine, which then marked the border between Maine and New Brunswick. In the short time they were married, she and John had six children. On 3 November 1817, John Low died of "consumption", leaving Miriam a widow at twenty-seven. She tried to maintain a life in Castine but finally, a year later, she returned to her family in Parrsboro where she met and married the Reverend Charles.

She was a good match for him, intelligent and thoughtful, particularly in matters of religion, and those who knew her say she could talk well and much. In addition to the six children she brought from her first marriage, Miriam bore four children as the wife of the Reverend Charles. There were three sons, Charles, born 2 July 1821; Nathan, born 18 July 1823;[10] and James, who died on 26 December 1825, twenty days after his birth. On 27 August 1829 they had a daughter, Charlotte (Charlotte was a favorite of her father and stayed at home to care for him after her mother died).

Education was valued in the Tupper home, and Charles began his education under his parents' tutelage. He later attended a school at which one of the teachers was Jonathon McCully. At the age of 15 he left school to work as an apprentice with Dr. Benjamin Page, an Amherst general practitioner who, as was usual at the time, included surgery in his practice.

Dr. Page advertised himself as *B.G. Page, Surgeon and Accoucheur (Twenty-two years standing)*. He indicated that he was a member of the Royal College of Surgeons, and offered medical and surgical advice for five shillings. He also offered a detailed list of his charges for such items as "Certificate of Health...5 shillings" and "Fee for advice, over three miles, 2 shillings per mile." An "ordinary case of Accouchement (medicines not charged)" cost one pound five shillings. He further announced that "In order to obviate any misconception relative to his terms as a General Practitioner, Dr. Page begs respectfully to inform the public of his minimum scale."

Charles's experience with Dr. Page excited him, and he soon knew that he wanted to be a physician. However, if he wanted to follow his desire he would have to acquire some formal education, an expensive proposition for a minister's son. His father knew that the road would not be easy, but he was also aware that his son had the determination to reach any goal he chose. Both father and son exhibited the qualities of "doggedness, a methodical manner of thinking and acting, and seriousness and gravity in respect of all duties."[11] In his journal, the Reverend Charles wrote, "Having decided on mature deliberation to give my son Charles an education in order that he might be prepared to enter the medical profession, on August 1, 1837, I sent him to our educational institution at Wolfville."

Wolfville, a small town in Kings County, Nova Scotia, is on the Cornwallis River, not far from Charles's home town. It was named for the DeWolf family, planters who had come to Nova Scotia from Connecticut in 1764. It was in Wolfville, on 1 May 1829, that the Baptists of the area opened Horton Academy, a school primarily, but not exclusively, for the education of young Baptist men who were considering careers in the ministry. The Academy eventually became Acadia University. For the young Tupper it provided the formal education he required to enable him to further his studies in medicine.

At Horton, Charles met young Daniel MacNeill Parker, and formed a friendship that would last a lifetime. Parker was descended from Loyalists; he was a charming young man, hard-working, intelligent, and mature beyond his years. He was also considering a career in medicine, and it is probable that his interest was intensified as a result of his friendship with Tupper.

There is one tangible memento in Wolfville of Tupper's and Parker's days at Horton. The two young men took part in planting ornamental trees on the Academy property. The trees were brought on flatbed boats down the Cornwallis River from the nearby town of Kentville and planted all around the grounds. Some of the trees were destroyed in a fire in 1877, and others were cut for various reasons, but some remain and one bears a plaque indicating that it was planted by Charles Tupper.[12]

Tupper was a brash, impetuous and fearless young man and had many brushes with death through his life. The first of these happened during his Horton days, when he was saved from drowning by a friend and fellow student named Pat Hockney. Charles, determined that it would not happen again, asked Hockney to teach him to swim.

After his studies at Horton, he set his sights on entering the medical college at Edinburgh University. Edinburgh was recognized as the finest medical school available, although by 1825 there were some fourteen medical schools in the United States and the British North American colonies, including Harvard, Pennsylvania and McGill. In fact, many of these schools had been based on the Edinburgh model and staffed by Edinburgh graduates. British colonies still looked to the mother country for the best in education. In the first half of the 19th century, some twenty-five physicians in Nova Scotia were Edinburgh trained, and many were medical leaders as well as leaders in communities at large.

There were obstacles. Four years at Edinburgh would be expensive, and the Tuppers were not wealthy. The transatlantic trip would take six weeks. The student would have to remain in Europe for the duration of his studies. When he set his mind to do something, however, he allowed nothing to stand in his way. He had already earned some money in small jobs and as a schoolteacher, and he knew that it might be possible to remove one year of study abroad if he could apprentice successfully with a prominent physician in Nova Scotia. Three years instead of four would relieve some of the financial pressure.

There were many possibilities. It was common for established physicians to take apprentices into their practices. The physician and the young apprentice, or more likely the apprentice's father, drew up and signed a considerable document indicating what would be expected from each. A fee was paid to the physician, who in turn provided training in medicine, and sometimes room and board.

His classmate Daniel MacNeill Parker had a similar medical education. He began his medical studies with the distinguished Halifax physician William Bruce Almon. When he was only 15 years old, his father and Dr. Almon signed an indenture of apprenticeship in which it was agreed, among other things, that young Daniel would remain for three years, would not frequent taverns or ale-houses, and would not marry. In return, Dr. Almon would "to the best of his power and ability, teach or instruct or cause to be taught or instructed, the said Daniel MacNeill Parker in the science, profession and practise of a physician, and the art and mystery of a surgeon, and the trade and business of an apothecary and druggist . . . ."[13] Daniel's father would pay Dr. Almon £100 for the instruction, and would also see to Daniel's room, board and clothing.

Tupper looked to Windsor, Nova Scotia, and to Dr. Ebenezer Fitch Harding. Tupper and Dr. Harding had much in common. Like Tupper, Harding was the eldest son of a Baptist minister. His father was the Reverend Theodore Seth Harding, one of the most influential men in the early Baptist ministry in Nova Scotia. Both Tupper and Harding were descended from New England planters. Dr Harding was named for his maternal grandfather, Ebenezer Fitch, who came to Nova Scotia from Windsor, Connecticut, and lived for some time in Amherst before moving to the Horton area. He had been educated in Halifax and at the University of New York, and was a member of the College of Physicians and Surgeons in New York. His wife was Sarah Bayard, and the Bayard family were well known in New Brunswick medical circles.

Tupper began his apprenticeship with Harding on 7 November 1839, and concluded it on 27 August 1840. During that time he lived at the Harding home and assisted in surgery and confinements as well as learning to compound medicines. He liked to tell the story of assisting Dr. Harding to amputate the leg of an Indian named Noel. Dr. Harding gave Tupper the leg for dissection, but he was soon approached by friends of Noel who said that the leg would have to be buried or else Noel would be a crippled man at resurrection and through all eternity. Tupper agreed. After dissecting the leg he carefully wrapped it and buried it in the Roman Catholic cemetery.

He got along well with Harding. At the conclusion of their time together he was given a certification of his apprenticeship which read:

Windsor, August 1840
These are to certify that Mr. Charles Tupper has been engaged
in the study of medicine under my direction from

November 7, 1839 to August 27, 1840. During this period, under my immediate notice, he has dissected, frequently compounded and dispensed medicines. He has often visited the sick with me and alone. I am highly satisfied with his abilities, correct moral deportment and with the zeal and diligence he has manifested in the prosecution of the various studies connected with the profession of medicine. I therefore cheerfully recommend him to the attention and kindness of all friends of good morals and of the healing art.

E.F. Harding, M.D. of the College of Physicians and Surgeons, New York.[14]

Money was still a problem, but Charles's uncle Nathan offered to help. Charles had often spent the Christmas holidays and weekends at his Uncle Nathan's home when his family was living in Fredericton.

He was 19 years old when he sailed from Nova Scotia. He had a small amount of money, some letters of introduction and a powerful determination to succeed. He was physically strong and fearless, impetuous and impatient. He had a clear intellect and a serious manner – some would say humourless – and people described him as being courteous and gentlemanly. He never backed down from a fight, and occasionally initiated them. The mate on the *Huntington*, a Mr. Brown, discovered this to his dismay on the outward voyage. Mr. Brown smoked a pipe, and he liked to smoke it upwind of Tupper. One morning, Tupper protested that it interfered with his bible reading but only received what he described as a surly response. "In an instant," said Tupper, "I smashed the bowl of his pipe against his jaw into a dozen pieces with a blow of my fist . . . the mate went to his bunk, which he only left on the third day after. The captain said I had done just right, and Mr. Brown gave me a wide berth from that time." Although he would only occasionally use his fists, it was a style that would characterize his career.

The remainder of the voyage was uneventful, if somewhat rough. It was a momentous time in his life and in the life of the British Empire. Young Queen Victoria, who had ascended the throne only three years before, married Prince Albert of Saxe-Coburg-Gotha in 1840, the year of Tupper's journey, and there was excitement in the air in Britain. Penny postage was established, the London Library and Kew Gardens were opened, and Nelson's column was erected in Trafalgar Square. Closer to home, Lower and Upper Canada were united by an Act of Parliament, and Lord Durham was named first Governor General of the newly united colonies. And in Nova Scotia a coalition government was in power, while Joseph Howe's row with the Nova Scotia Baptists was just heating up.

Before long the *Huntington* arrived in Glasgow and Charles took a stagecoach to Edinburgh.

Chapter 1 – Notes

1. Tupper, The Rt. Hon. Sir Charles, Bart., GCMG; *Recollections of Sixty Years*; Cassell and Company Ltd.; London, New York, Toronto and Melbourne; 1914; p. 2.

2. The village is now called Warren.

3. According to the History of the First Baptist Church in Amherst, Miriam Lockhart Lowe was a young widow with five children when she married the Rev. Charles.

4. The Reverend Charles's mother, the former Elizabeth West, was reputed to be a woman of extraordinary talents, and a number of her descendants, including the Rev. Charles and her grandson, the missionary Rev. Silas Tertius Rand, were linguists.

5. *The History of Kings County, Nova Scotia.* Eaton., p. 536.

6. His obituary (*Amherst Gazette*, January 21, 1881) said that he was a balanced personality, true to the moral code he preached, "cautious and enterprising; merciful and just; firm in his belief yet courteous to those who differed from him." It was also noted that he was not a good orator, being knowledgeable, but dull.

7. The Acadians had been expelled from Nova Scotia because the governor was concerned that they would not be loyal to the monarch. Some escaped to other parts of the maritime provinces, but many were put aboard ships and sent to Louisiana. Their descendants are the Louisiana "Cajuns".

8. According to the Tupper Genealogy, Sir Charles Tupper wrote to Gladstone in 1867, "As to my indignant Protestantism, consider that I come of martyr's blood--of confessor's certainly, according to family tradition – and that I must always deliver my conscience."

9. Miriam Lockhart was born in Parrsboro on 16 January 1790, the daughter of James and Miriam Wadkins (Knowlton) Lockhart.

10. Nathan married Eleanor Jane Bent (1829-1919) on 18 September 1847. They had seven children: Clara Minnie; Flora (Nelson); Edgar (m. Julia Trites); Ella (Chapman); Sophia; Ida (Robb); and Charles Osborne (m. 1st Elizabeth robbins, 2nd Charlotte Burdette). Charles became a physician and practised in Brooklyn, New York.

11. Longley, J.W.; *The Makers of Canada Series, Charles Tupper*; Makers of Canada (Morang)Ltd.; Toronto; 1916; (Parkman Edition).

12. The tree can be found along the main street at the bottom of the lawn in front of the old administration building.

13. Parker, William Frederick; *Daniel McNeill Parker, M.D., His Ancestry and a Memoir of His Life*; William Briggs; Toronto; 1910. p. 94.

14. Tupper Papers, Public Archives of Nova Scotia, document # 5.

CHAPTER 2

Edinburgh

C harles had hardly left home when his mother wrote to him, "My very dear Son – you are constantly in my mind; and I would make almost any sacrifice that was in my power to see you."[1] But the Edinburgh adventure had begun, and Miriam Tupper would not see her son for three years.

When Charles arrived in Edinburgh one of the letters he carried was from his parents to James Ratchford DeWolf, a senior medical student. James was the son of the Hon. Thomas Andrew Strange DeWolf, the Member of Provincial Parliament for Kings County, N.S., and a member of the first Executive Council of the Province of Nova Scotia. Like Charles, James had attended Horton Academy and had apprenticed with Dr. Harding in Windsor. He was three years older than Charles and two years ahead of him in medical studies. James immediately invited him to share his lodgings at the home of a Mrs. Innes, 5 South College Street. This friendship would bring them together in many ventures throughout their lives.

Having secured a place to stay, Tupper applied to the Senate of the University to request that his apprenticeship with Dr. Page and Dr. Harding count as a year of medical study which would enable him to graduate in three years rather than the usual four. The Senate agreed, and he wrote and passed his matriculation exams. Thus his studies at the University of Edinburgh began. They were to be exciting and memorable years, a time when he would come under the influence of some inspiring faculty who would broaden his view of the world and his vision of the future.

Charles knew he could look forward to a medical education that was respected throughout the world, and although in retrospect some would say Edinburgh was then past its peak and beginning to decline in importance, it would be because of the rise of other institutions rather than because of any lessening of Edinburgh's fine medical system. It was not by chance that the University of Edinburgh was held in such universal esteem. Education was of great importance to the people of Scotland. John Knox had encouraged universal education, stressing freedom of thought, freedom of speech and freedom of action. St. Andrew's University had been set up in 1411, Glasgow in 1451, Aberdeen in 1495, and Edinburgh in 1583. In theory, education was open to all. In fact, the financial cost and the usual prejudices against women kept enrolment open largely to middle and upper class males.[2] Education was also closely tied to religion in the major universities in England, but there was no requirement to adhere to any one particular religion in Scottish universities. This openness encouraged a wide mix of scholars and students to come to Edinburgh, and many of the young Tupper's professors were outstanding scholars, well-known to historians of medicine. In the manner of the best teachers they would provide him not only with medical skills and information but would also be his role models. He would learn physiology and surgery, but he would also learn that poverty, lack of education and ill health go hand-in-hand. He would learn the importance of a good public health system, the desirability of maintaining health statistics and the necessity of taking a stand to effect positive change, even when the opposition is strong.

Tupper's Teachers

As always, of course, there are exceptions to the rule, as Tupper learned in his first term anatomy class. His professor was Alexander Monro tertius, the third of the family to occupy the chair of anatomy at Edinburgh. This Monro's grandfather, Alexander Monro primus, had studied at Leyden and had brought the methods of the European schools back to Scotland. The excellence of his teaching and the excitement of anatomy in the understanding of medicine brought Edinburgh's reputation to a peak. His son, Alexander Monro secundus, succeeded his famous father, and his son, Alexander Monro tertius, completed the dynasty. Unfortunately, the third Monro was a rather dull and lacklustre teacher, given to slow and ponderous reading of the lecture material prepared by his father and grandfather. His grandfather's lectures had been written a century before, but he read them verbatim, including the introduction, "When I was a student in Leyden in 1719. . . ." Because of this, students often paid their university fees for Monro's lectures, but took their actual instruction in anatomy from teachers outside the university. Some have suggested that the wide recognition of the excellence of Edinburgh came with primus and faded with tertius.

Charles was taught practical anatomy by a Mr. Richard J. McKenzie, a young surgeon-anatomist who lectured at the Surgeons' Hall. His chemistry professor was Professor Charles Hope. Hope liked teaching and was a good and popular teacher, his classes sometimes numbering over 500 students. He had studied in France with Lavoisier and had corresponded with John Dalton, the English chemist and physicist who had introduced the atomic theory into chemistry. He himself had done some noted experiments on the expansion of water as it freezes. The students liked Hope and they were impressed that his chemistry experiments always worked in his class demonstrations.

Charles later told a story of studying long and hard for his chemistry examination, the only subject about which he had some concern. The studying was not going well, so he went to see Mr. Kemp, one of Hope's assistants, to ask for a preliminary examination. Kemp examined Charles, and said he was sure he would do well. As he was leaving, Kemp said in passing, "Professor Hope has, during the past three weeks, spent much time experimenting upon sodium and potassium and their compounds." Charles immediately went home, and spent the rest of the day studying sodium and potassium. On the day of the examination he went into Hope's room, and Hope's first question was, "Mr. Tupper, what is sodium?" Charles launched into a twenty minute discussion of sodium and potassium and their compounds as Professor Hope nodded his approval. Eventually, Professor Hope rose from his chair and said, "Mr. Tupper I have the pleasure of congratulating you on passing a most satisfactory examination." He wrote *Optime* beside Tupper's name on the student list and, Tupper said, "sent me on my way, rejoicing."[3]

But Charles's most illustrious teacher that first term was one of the outstanding medical figures of his time, Dr. James Young Simpson, who taught him midwifery. Simpson was of working class background, born in 1811 in the Scottish town of Bathgate. His family supported him financially and otherwise, as he studied in Edinburgh. While a student he was so profoundly disturbed by the screams of pain of women during childbirth that he considered giving up the study of medicine. Instead, he determined to find some method of controlling and easing the pain. After many experiments, some on members of his own family and his friends as well as on himself, he began to use chloroform during deliveries. Simpson, newly appointed to the chair of midwifery, was Charles's favorite teacher.

In his second term, the spring of 1841, Tupper studied natural history under Professor Robert Jameson. Jameson had studied in Freiburg under the geologist Abraham Werner and in his lectures taught geology and mineralogy as well as meteorology and zoology. The same spring of 1841 Charles began to do ward work at the Edinburgh Royal Infirmary.

Many of Charles's teachers were not only learned in the sciences but had broad and impressive backgrounds in other areas. For instance, Professor Thomas Stewart Traill taught him medical jurisprudence. Traill was an Edinburgh graduate who had spent some time in practice in Liverpool where he was a founder of the Literary and Philosophical Society of that city, and was also involved in the founding of the Royal Institute and the Liverpool Mechanics Institute. A man of broad interests, he had edited the eighth edition of the Encyclopaedia Britannica. His chair in forensic medicine included studies in public health.

Professor Graham was Charles's professor of botany and was also one of the physicians under whom Tupper worked at the Royal Infirmary. Graham liked to take his students on daylong excursions on the weekends through the surrounding countryside. Tupper enjoyed these trips, although they began early in the morning and concluded around midnight. His friend Dan Parker didn't particularly enjoy them, nor was he overly fond of Professor Graham. Since the excursions were not obligatory, Dan skipped them to study things he thought were more important. At examination time the

Professor asked questions which could only have been discovered on the excursions and, since Parker was unable to answer, he failed. He pleaded his case to the University Senate, who agreed that no student should be held responsible for information provided only on non-obligatory excursions, and Professor Graham's decision was reversed. Parker passed the exam and the year.[4]

Parker was happy to accompany Tupper on other excursions, however. He recounted to his son years later how he and Charles liked to ramble through the historic city on Sundays, ignoring the strictures of Scottish sabbatarianism of the period. One Sunday they were swinging down the High Street, whistling as they went, when they were noticed by a small boy, who gazed at them open-mouthed, and said, "What! Whustlin' on the Sabbuth!"

Charles's education was broadened in many other ways during his sojourn in Edinburgh. He had arrived with a letter of introduction to another Dr. Graham, who lived in the Edinburgh suburb of Newington. Graham took a personal interest in the young student from Nova Scotia, and Charles dined with him and his wife every Saturday afternoon at four. It was at the Grahams' home that he reluctantly had his first taste of Scotch whisky. He knew his father would have frowned, or worse, since he was a leader in the temperance movement in Nova Scotia. It was also with the Grahams that Charles first attended the theatre. Again, he went with some misgivings (and perhaps some hesitation, because his father also had a loathing for the theatre). He saw a performance of *The Lady of Lyons* with Charles Kean and Ellen Tree. He said later, "From the moment the curtain rose and Kean rushed forward . . . I was entranced." He added, "It was a startling reality, and I felt that I would sacrifice anything to be a Kean."[5] Tupper would, of course, play on a larger stage, and would have plenty of opportunity to show his own impressive dramatic flair.

James DeWolfe graduated in August 1841, and returned to Nova Scotia. Tupper decided to change his lodgings and moved to Mrs. Wilson's home at 19 Salisbury Street, where he shared the rooms of John Smith of Manchester. Mrs. Wilson's was a favorite place for medical students. Her lodgers included Edward Bowman, the son of Captain Bowman, who had been Governor of Allahabad, and Tupper's old friend from Nova Scotia, Daniel McNeill Parker.

Also at Mrs. Wilson's was a Portuguese student from Madeira named Da Costa. He was sharing Dan Parker's rooms and was jealous of the close friendship between Parker and Tupper. In addition, Tupper, in his usual brash and impetuous way, had insulted Da Costa by mimicking his heavily accented English. William Frederick Parker, writing in his father's biography, reported an incident when the two clashed. One evening, Da Costa, "livid with rage," rushed in and grabbed a loaded pistol which he always kept in his bureau drawer. He ran from the room and headed for Tupper's room. Parker realized what was happening, yelled to Tupper, and ran down the hall after Da Costa. He arrived just in time to see the pistol pointed at Tupper's head. Parker jumped him from behind, and Tupper sprang across the desk and tackled from the front. The three went to the floor in a fierce struggle, and Parker managed to tear the pistol from his hand, while Tupper "choked him into submission." Tupper apologized profusely to the chagrined Da Costa for having insulted him, and Da Costa was apparently satisfied. He left Mrs. Wilson's lodgings the next day, but the pistol stayed behind in Parker's locked trunk. Once again, Tupper's life had been saved by a friend.[6]

His Edinburgh friends included a Dr. Gordon from Pictou, Nova Scotia, who had graduated in medicine from Edinburgh in 1841. Gordon married and set up practice in Edinburgh and welcomed his Nova Scotian expatriate friends in his home. Tupper and Parker also spent several weeks in Newcastle at the home of Captain Arthur, the uncle and guardian of their friend Bowman. They formed a warm and strong friendship which lasted until Captain Arthur's death.

Mrs. Davidson, formerly from Halifax, Nova Scotia, who had married and was living in Edinburgh, also welcomed the two young medical students into her home. They became friends of her two nieces, Sophia Almon and Emma Almon of Halifax, who were also studying in Edinburgh. Tupper writes of having accompanied the ladies to see Queen Victoria and Prince Albert on their visit to the city. The crush of the crowd was great and it was difficult to see, so Tupper and Sophia climbed to the top of an omnibus for a better view. It was his first view of the young monarch, who would play an important role in his life and by whom he would one day be knighted.

Tupper and Parker often spent their Sundays walking in Edinburgh and its surroundings. Medical students were, at the time, considered to be a wild and unruly lot, but both young Nova Scotians were ambitious and determined to do well in their profession, and although they enjoyed their days in the beautiful city, they studied hard and apparently avoided the wilder escapades of their confreres.

During the academic year 1841-42, Tupper came under the influence of two of the more interesting medical men of the time, Dr. William Pulteney Alison and Dr. Robert Christison. Dr. Alison was professor of physiology. He was the son of an Episcopalian clergyman, and was a philosopher-physician who had graduated from Edinburgh. His lectures in the Institute of Medicine had been collected into a book called "Outlines of Physiology", but he was most celebrated for his work among the poor. He was concerned about what he termed "the utter inadequacy of private benevolence." Just two years before, he had published a stinging criticism of the Scottish Poor Law. He wrote (in part):

Let us look to the closes of Edinburgh, and the wynds of Glasgow, and thoroughly understand the character and habits, the diseases and mortality, of the unemployed poor, unprotected by the law, who gather there from all parts of the country; let us study the condition of the aged and disabled poor in all the smaller towns in Scotland; let us listen to the tales of misery which come to us from the remote parts of the Highlands and Islands . . . let us compare these things with the provisions for the poor, not only in England but in many other Christian countries; and so far from priding ourselves on the smallness of the sums which are applied to this purpose in Scotland . . . we must honestly and candidly confess, that our parsimony in this particular is equally injurious to the poor and discreditable to the rich in Scotland.[7]

Alison had begun his medical career as physician to the New Town Dispensary, and it was there that he learned how poverty obviously encouraged the spread of disease, particularly in epidemics like cholera and smallpox. From his example, Tupper learned lessons which he would one day use in his approach to education and health care in Nova Scotia.

Dr. Robert Christison was Tupper's professor of materia medica. He was the son of a professor of latin at the university, who had graduated in medicine from Edinburgh and studied at St. Bartholomew's Hospital in London, and with Robiquet in Paris before returning to Edinburgh to take the chair of medical jurisprudence. He was a much published expert on poisons, and was a prominent witness in criminal cases, including the infamous Burke and Hare case. His knowledge of chemistry and toxicology led him to publish a "*Dispensatory*" in 1842, and he was the chairman of the committee of the General Medical Council which published the first Pharmacopoeia of Great Britain and Ireland in 1864.

The newly appointed William Henderson was Tupper's professor of pathology. A few years later, Henderson became the centre of a storm of controversy when he announced that he had become a disciple of homoeopathic medicine. But in addition to Simpson, Alison and Christison, the major influences in Tupper's final years at Edinburgh were two great surgeons, James Miller and James Syme.

Miller took the chair of surgery in 1842. He was a skilled surgeon, and had written two popular textbooks on the subject. But Miller was also known for his ability as an orator, both as a University lecturer and in the public arena. Tupper was in Edinburgh during the Disruption of the Scottish Church in 1843, when Miller wrote and spoke with passion and wit on behalf of the Free Church of Scotland.

James Syme was an outstanding surgeon. He was also a quarrelsome man with an acrimonious and unforgiving disposition, and he was refused the chair of surgery at the Royal Infirmary. Fortunately, he came from a relatively wealthy family and, though only 30 years old at the time, his wealth and his considerable reputation as a surgeon enabled him to buy an old mansion called Minto House to establish a surgical hospital for himself. It was a tremendous success, and its reputation came to rival that of the Royal Infirmary. In 1833, he was appointed Professor of Clinical Surgery at Edinburgh.

Tupper spent some time as resident house surgeon at Minto House Hospital. When he left, he "received a flattering testimonial from the physicians." But he also had occasion to visit Syme as a patient. There were two maiden ladies in Edinburgh, a Miss Patterson and a Miss Tulloch who had a house in Warriston Crescent and who frequently entertained celebrities who visited the city, as well as students from the university. Tupper met some distinguished men and women at these soirees, but one night, when he was leaving Warriston Crescent, he fell and bruised the elbow of his right arm. He tells the story in his *Life and Letters*:

"The joint inflamed; it was leeched, and ultimately counter-irritation was used. When writing my graduation essay it became troublesome. I went over one morning to consult Mr. Syme, the great professor of surgery of that day. He was standing on one leg with an elbow on the mantelpiece. I flexed my elbow, saying 'Do you hear that creaking sound?' He flexed his knee-joint, saying: 'Do you hear that? If you will cure my knee, I will cure your elbow, but I am afraid we will both have to leave it to time.'"

Tupper studied midwifery in his final year, again under Dr. J.Y. Simpson. He decided to compete for the gold medal offered for the best graduation thesis. Tupper's thesis was *The Mechanism and Management of Parturition*. He did not receive the gold medal, but in *Life and Letters* he says that he was told by Dr. Simpson that he might have received a medal had not another gold medal already been given in midwifery. Apparently the awarding committee thought it unsuitable to present two gold medals in the same area.[9]

In the *Tupper Papers* there is a letter from Dr. Simpson:[10]

Dr. Tupper was a most delightful student during the period of his medical studies at the University of Edinburgh. He has gone through a most complete medical education and is most intimately conversant with all the departments of his profession. I can speak more especially of Dr. Tupper's thorough knowledge of midwifery, a branch in which he has had extensive practice while resident in Edinburgh. His graduation thesis was one relating to obstetric practice. It contained an account of upwards of 100 cases of labour that he had attended. It was so minute and masterly in its details that I recommended it to the Medical Faculty as worthy of one of the University's Gold Medals. Altogether, when I consider Dr. Tupper's innate assiduity and love of his profession, his kind, quiet and gentlemanly manners, and his perfect knowledge of medicine and surgery, I can entertain no doubt of his ultimate success and fame as a medical practitioner.

signed J.Y. Simpson, M.D.

Professor of Midwifery in the University of Edinburgh etc. etc.
22 Albany Street Edinburgh
10 August, 1843

It was time for final exams and graduation. Most students did both university examinations and the examinations for membership in the Royal College of Edinburgh. Tupper had planned to do only the university exams because he couldn't afford the courses for the Royal College exams. Captain Arthur, Bowman's guardian, had asked Tupper why he wasn't taking the Royal College exams and Tupper pointed out that he needed only the MD to practise in Nova Scotia and, frankly, couldn't afford to do the extra courses. Arthur, who was a wealthy ship-owner, insisted that Tupper borrow the money from him and refused to take his note. He told him that if he (Arthur) died, the note might be called in when it was not convenient for Tupper. Tupper accepted the Captain's generosity and in all received one hundred and twenty-five pounds.[10]

In a document dated 24 April 1843, Tupper's professors, Traill, Simpson, Henderson, Miller, Alison and Christison awarded him B (Bene) or B.B. and he passed with a Second Class. For the privilege he paid £20.16.

The actual conferring of the degree was to take place on August 1, so Tupper was left with about three months and a little of Captain Arthur's money. He decided to travel to London and Paris. He made friends as he went, who in turn introduced him to others. He thoroughly enjoyed the travel and his appetite for distant places was whetted. It would continue on both sides of the Atlantic until he was well into his nineties.

When he returned to Edinburgh he and Ned Bowman stayed with Captain Arthur until graduation. Following graduation, he made a three week tour of the Highlands with Dan Parker and two older female friends, a Mrs. Murray and her sister Mrs. McKonnichie.

It was the end of August, 1843. For three years Tupper had studied under some of the great physicians of the time. He had travelled and met people of different nationalities, old and young, wealthy and poor. He had lived in and visited the cities of Scotland as well London and Paris, and he had hiked through the countryside. He had eagerly sought out interesting experiences, having his fortune told by gypsies, allowing himself to be "magnetised" on stage by a travelling magician, travelling through the Highlands by donkey. His life had been threatened, and he had risked his life to save a young man who had fallen through the ice of a loch while skating. He had made friendships which would last a lifetime and cemented other friendships which had begun in Nova Scotia with men like Dan Parker and James DeWolfe, and with women such as Emma and Sophie Almon. But he had graduated and it was time to go home and establish a practice and a living. He sailed from Glasgow on a barque carrying pig iron. Parker and several other friends came to see him off. He said, "I started for home, more homesick at leaving Edinburgh than I had ever been."[11]

Chapter 2 – Notes

1. From an article written for the *Canadian Messenger* by Miriam's husband, Charles. The Archives of the Cumberland County Museum RG1-17; 79-5-453.

2. Edinburgh's first female student in medicine was Sophia Jex-Blake, who matriculated in 1869. Her acceptance prompted a storm of protest from students and professors. In 1870, some male students attempted to stop women from attending anatomy lectures, an event called the Surgeon's Hall Riot. The controversy concluded with court action.

3. *The Life and Letters of the Rt. Hon. Sir Charles Tupper Bart., K.C.M.G.* E.M. Saunders (ed.). New York. Frederick A. Stokes Co. 1916. Vol. 1, p.17.

4. Parker, William Frederick; *Daniel McNeill Parker, M.D., His Ancestry and a Memoir of His Life*; Toronto. William Briggs. 1910.

5. *The Life and Letters of the Rt. Hon. Sir Charles Tupper Bart., K.C.M.G.* Vol 1, p. 12.

6. Parker, William Frederick; *Daniel McNeill Parker, M.D., His Ancestry and a Memoir of His Life*; Toronto. William Briggs. 1910; p. 104.

7. W.P. Alison, *Observations on the Management of the Poor In Scotland and its Effects on the Health of the Great Towns*, second edition (Edinburgh, 1840) p. 66; quoted in *People and Society in Scotland*, Volume II, 1830-1914; edited by W. Hamish Fraser and R.J. Morris, John Donald Publishers Ltd, Edinburgh, 1990; p. 265.

8. *The Life and Letters of the Rt. Hon. Sir Charles Tupper;* Vol. 1 p. 18.

9. Ibid p. 10.

10. Five years later, when Tupper was in practice in Amherst, he heard that Captain Arthur's financial affairs had taken a sharp downturn. He immediately repaid the one hundred and twenty pounds with 6% interest. In his *Life*, he points out that had he given Arthur his note, the money would have gone not to Arthur, but to his creditors.

11. *The Life and Letters of the Rt. Hon Sir Charles Tupper*, Vol. 1, p. 27.

CHAPTER 3

Country Doctor

The barque took fifty-four days to make its way from Glasgow to Boston, and Tupper was seasick for all but the last week of the journey. He quickly booked another ship from Boston to Saint John, and from there returned to his father's home in Amherst.

The Amherst to which the twenty-two year old Tupper returned was the centre of a thriving farming community near the border of the sister colony of New Brunswick. The area had originally been inhabited by the native people, a number of the surrounding settlements having since kept their descriptive Indian names. Later, much of the farmland had been reclaimed and farmed by the Acadians. After the expulsion of the Acadians by Governor Lawrence in 1755, the land was given to Planters from New England and, after the American Revolutionary War, to Loyalists and disbanded soldiers from New England. Some of the new settlers were given lands to farm, but it wasn't necessary for them to have been experienced farmers. The term "Planter" by which the New England group was known came from the Elizabethan term for colonists. They were people who planted colonies.

The area around was still heavily forested, mostly pine, spruce and hemlock, and a lumber industry was developing. The woods were also full of game and there was plentiful fishing in the waters nearby. A small shipbuilding industry was beginning in a number of communities.

Although funds were allotted for the building of roads as early as 1795, they were still rough and most of them could be travelled only on horseback and not by wagon. The mail system was still a rather primitive affair, and mail was carried by wagon along the main roads. There was a road known as the Post Road from Saint John, New Brunswick, to Halifax, and a stagecoach went from Truro to Dorchester in New Brunswick carrying both passengers and mail. The coach stopped at inns which were about ten miles apart to allow a change of horses, which could then set off at a gallop for the next stopping place.

The young Charles Tupper, local boy, son of a respected cleric, descended from a well-known, if not wealthy, Planter family, was welcomed back to his community. Many years later an early biographer, J.W. Longley, said, "Tupper's chief means of securing the confidence and enthusiasm of his associates were earnestness, directness, courage, and innate force. In his palmy days his personality was almost commanding. He was industrious and indefatigable; whoever else reposed, Tupper never rested upon his oars. His friends had faith in his resources, and confidence in his ability to meet at all times any situation which confronted him."[1] These qualities served him well in the communities he cared for as a general practitioner. In addition, he was a good looking young man, a little shorter than medium height, with thick black hair, and an air of strength, a sense of confidence and tremendous energy. Add an education at Europe's chief medical school by some of the best medical professors of the time and it was no wonder that he very quickly built a thriving medical and surgical practice from Malagash to Parrsboro, covering most of Cumberland County.

When he opened his practice in 1843 in Amherst, he started a pharmacy on Church St. which continues to this day, the longest running pharmacy in Canada.[2]

There had been about sixty physicians in Nova Scotia at the beginning of the nineteenth century, and Tupper's old mentor, Dr. Page, was still practising in Amherst when he returned. There were fifteen physicians in Halifax, almost all Edinburgh graduates, and Tupper had given some consideration to joining them in the city. But, as his old friend Dan Parker wrote from Edinburgh to another mutual friend, John Smith, "he considered a bird in the hand worth two in the bush, and relinquished that plan," and stayed in Amherst where he was known and welcomed.

Parker thought it was a wise move on Tupper's part. "He has been very successful, and is even sporting a carriage and pair. I hear from him often, and he informed me not long since that his receipts for his first year's practise amounted to nearly £400, with which he furnished a house and provided all the et ceteras for a wife. A lady and gentleman from Amherst spent a month in Edinburgh this winter and informed me that he is clearing the field and taking the cream of the practise from his older brethern."[3]

The letter was written on 10 February 1845, but Tupper did not marry until 8 October 1846. His bride was Frances Amelia Morse, the daughter of Silas Hibbert and Elizabeth (Stewart) Morse of Amherst. Her great-grandfather, Joseph Morse, had come to Cumberland County from Dedham, Massachusetts, in 1763, and her grandfather, Alpheus, had been one of three original settlers on the Amherst land. Her paternal grandmother was Theodora Crane whose father, Major Silas Crane, a Loyalist, had come to Nova Scotia from Connecticut in 1761.

Alpheus, however, was not a Loyalist, at least not during the attack on Fort Cumberland in 1776. During that siege many New Englanders who had re-located to Nova Scotia, including future Nova Scotia Attorney-General Richard Uniacke, decided that they were not neutral Yankees after all but were, in fact, patriots to the American cause. When the siege of the Fort failed, the "patriots" were rounded up. Alpheus was taken to a jail in Halifax and his wife and children had to rely on the mercy of compassionate soldiers at the Fort. Later, when a general amnesty was declared, Alpheus and Uniacke were released. Alpheus, returning to his Cumberland home, became a justice of the peace and a pillar of the community.[4] Alpheus and Theodora had three sons, the Hon. James Morse, a lawyer and member of the Legislative Assembly, W.A.D. Morse, a Judge, and Frances's father, Silas Hibbert Morse, prothonotary of the Supreme Court of Nova Scotia.

Frances's mother was Elizabeth Stewart. Elizabeth was born in Halifax, the daughter of James Stewart, who had come to Nova Scotia from Scotland in 1790, and Elizabeth Bremner. Frances's uncle was the Hon. Alexander Stewart, C.B., Master of the Rolls and

Judge of the Court of Vice-Admiralty. Alexander had practised law in Amherst and had represented Cumberland County in the Nova Scotia House of Assembly from 1826 to 1838. It was Alexander who provided young Dr. Tupper with his first opportunity to participate in the political life of Nova Scotia.

It was October, 1844, and Alexander Stewart had come to Amherst from Halifax to attend the wedding of his daughter. Joseph Howe arrived in Amherst at the same time and a meeting was set up so that Stewart and Howe might engage in a political debate. Tupper attended the meeting, and as soon as it was over he got on his horse and rode twenty miles to see a patient who had tetanus. He remained the night with his patient returning to Amherst the next day. He met Alexander Stewart who said that he had noticed that Tupper had paid close attention to what had transpired; he asked if he would write a report of the meeting to the leader of the Conservative Party. Tupper wrote a long, detailed and insightful report of the meeting and sent it to the Hon. J.W. Johnstone. It had been his first meeting with Joseph Howe, but it would not be his last. As Stephen Leacock pointed out, "He was Joseph Howe's great rival in a province that never had room for both of them."[5] The next decades would resound with the clash of these two very different personalities.

Frances was obviously used to the pros and cons of life in a political family. But she had married, not a politician, but a busy country doctor. They moved into a large Amherst house recently built by Silas Morse where their first child, Emma, was born just nine months later, followed in April, 1849, by another daughter, Elizabeth Stewart, called Lillie. Tupper's practice continued to grow. He rode long distances in all kinds of weather on still primitive roads. He sometimes stopped in at a friend's stable to change horses when his own tired before he had reached his destination. It was said that a farmer could always tell when the young doctor was out on a call because he would find a strange horse in the stable in place of his own. A doctor who had known him said that he had become widely known both for his professional skill and his willingness to answer any call, no matter how distant. In fact, he followed the prescription of his old mentor Dr. Page, who had indicated that the secret of success was to "know your business and attend to it, and thus make it the Interest of Society to employ you. This is real self-reliance. It confers true dignity as well as pecuniary personal independence on its possessor. . . ."

But there were difficult times. When Lillie was just six weeks old the house which the Tuppers shared with the Morses burned to the ground. The following year, Lillie suffered an attack of "diarrhoea caused by teething," probably acute gastroenteritis, and died suddenly. Tupper's mother, Miriam Lockhart Lowe Tupper, died in July of the following year, while her husband was away making arrangements to move to another parish in Annapolis County.

Tupper himself became ill with a serious attack of typhus he believed he had caught from a patient. He recognized the symptoms as he rode home, and as soon as he arrived he called for Dr. Page and shortly fell into a delirium. When he was recovering, but still feeling rather weak, he went out on a call to see a patient in Minudie. His horse fell overboard from the scow used as a ferry across the river. Tupper held the reins close to the horse's jaws, when "the ferryman, in gybing the sail, touched his hocks, and before I could let go, he had carried me overboard and we went down together. Fearing he would strike me with his feet, I let go of the bridle and dived deeper. When I came up, I was thirty or forty feet from the scow and my horse more than fifty yards distant." He and the horse swam to shore, but it was April and Tupper was severely chilled. He was taken to the house of Amos Seaman where he was put to bed "with warm blankets and a stiff tumbler of brandy and water [was] administered." After a couple of hours sleep, he recovered and went on his way.

He once fell asleep at a patient's house and couldn't be wakened for four hours. He had just finished a fifty mile horseback ride and a hundred mile drive in a wagon, on three separate calls to care for seriously ill patients in various corners of the county. He performed amputations in the patients' homes, sat beside children with scarlet fever, and sewed up lacerations caused by farm implements. It was the typical life of a country practitioner in mid-nineteenth century Nova Scotia.

The Tuppers' first son, born in October 1851, was called James Stewart, after Frances's grandfather. In August 1855, their second son, Charles Hibbert, was born. And it was in 1855 that Dr. Tupper, the young Edinburgh educated country doctor from Amherst, began a second career, one that would be momentous not only for him, but also for his province and country.

Chapter 3 – Notes

1. Longley, J.W.; *Sir Charles Tupper.* Toronto. Makers of Canada (Morang) Ltd. 1916: (Parkman Edition) p. 255.

2. The pharmacy started by Dr. Tupper has continued in the same location, but in various structures up to today. A few years after starting the pharmacy, Charles shared a partnership in the store with his brother Nathan who had by then obtained a medical degree. When Charles left for Halifax a few years later, Nathan continued the shop, taking in a clerk, R. C. Fuller, who had immigrated from England. Fuller bought the business from Nathan in 1875, and in 1882 took in John W. Morrison as an apprentice. Morrison later took his degree and the gold medal from the Philadelphia College of Pharmacy and returned as a partner to Fuller. The name changed to R. C. Fuller and Co. When Fuller died in 1936, B. T. Pugsley, who had been with the firm for 10 years, entered into partnership with Mr. Morrison, and the name Pugsley's Pharmacy continues over the door. (Pugsley documents, Cumberland Museum, Amherst N.S., RG 2, 79.7.9 and 79.7.11.)

3. Public Archives of Nova Scotia; *The Tupper Papers*, reel 11091 Doc. 2.

4. Clarke, Ernest A.; "Cumberland Planters and the Aftermath of the Attack on Fort Cumberland" from *They Planted Well*, a conference on New England Planters in Maritime Canada, edited by Margaret Conrad, Acadiensis Press, Fredericton, New Brunswick, 1988. pp. 53 and 60.

5. Leacock, Stephen; *Canada - The Foundations of its Future.* Privately printed in Montreal, Canada by the House of Seagram, 1941; p. 152.

CHAPTER 4

Political Life Begins

Charles Tupper's initial foray into the political arena in Nova Scotia took place in March of 1852. The year before, the prominent Liberal politician, Joseph Howe, and Mr. Fulton, a Conservative, had both been elected in Cumberland County by acclamation. It was a compromise agreement for each party to have a representative, until the Conservatives discovered that Fulton planned to abandon his party and join Howe and the Liberals. The hue and cry that followed Fulton's move resulted in the unseating of both members, and a new election was called for March, 1852.

Howe and Fulton stood as Liberal candidates, and the Conservatives chose A. MacFarlane and Thomas Andrew DeWolfe. The DeWolfes were descended from three cousins who had come as Planters to Nova Scotia from Connecticut, many of whom had taken their place in the public life of the colony. Thomas Andrew DeWolfe was a Halifax business man and a Methodist preacher.

On the evening before DeWolfe's nomination was to take place, young Dr. Tupper rode to River Philip to meet him and was asked if he would introduce him to the group who had gathered in the schoolhouse. It was Tupper's first speech on the political stage, and it impressed DeWolfe enough that he asked Tupper to make the speech proposing him as a candidate at the nomination meeting the next morning.

Tupper agreed, but he admitted years later that he was terrified at the prospect of making such a public speech. "I did not sleep much that night" he wrote, "and was so nervous the next morning that I threw up my breakfast on the way to the corner where the nomination was to take place."[1]

The people of Nova Scotia have always taken their politics seriously, and there was a huge gathering awaiting Dr. Tupper. They were somewhat surprised when "our young doctor," as they called him, rose to speak. Having proposed the nomination of Thomas DeWolfe, he began a criticism of Howe's policies. At that point Howe himself rose and approached the platform. Tupper immediately offered to give way to Howe's proposer since Howe was the former member. At first Howe demurred and told Tupper to go on, but he very quickly realized that the young doctor's forceful speech would be damaging to the Liberal cause, and he interrupted again. The assembly began to shout its disapproval, and the arguing went on for an hour before a committee decided that the candidates should speak first, followed by Tupper and the others.

DeWolfe and MacFarlane lost the election to the Liberals Howe and Fulton, but that nomination day in River Philip in March of 1852 marked not only the beginning of the political career of Charles Tupper, but also a rivalry between two great leaders, Joseph Howe and Charles Tupper, which would continue for the next two decades.

Charles Tupper and Joseph Howe were two very different men. Tupper was the son of a Baptist minister of Planter stock, whose family had come to Nova Scotia by choice in 1761. Howe's father, John Howe, was a Loyalist of Puritan stock who came to Nova Scotia with his young wife after being driven out of Massachusetts because he sided with the British. He was a printer, and when he came to Nova Scotia he was rewarded with the prestigious but low-paying offices of King's Printer and Postmaster-General.

Tupper's father was self-educated and Charles's education began at home, but he later attended Horton Academy in Wolfville and Medical School in Edinburgh. He was well-educated and had travelled extensively. Howe had to leave school at the age of thirteen to work as printer's devil in his father's print shop. His education continued at home and at the print shop where he read everything he could. He was well-versed in the classics and had a tremendous respect for the importance of education but, as one of his early biographers, William Lawson Grant, pointed out, "A thorough intellectual training would have done much for him...The discipline of a university career enables even a young man to know somewhat of his own strengths and weaknesses, especially somewhat of his own awful ignorance; and self-knowledge leads to self-control."[2]

When, in 1852, they first clashed, Howe was 47 years old and an established politician, prominent and highly respected in the province. Tupper was a young doctor, new to the business of politics, and just 30 years old. But the two men were separated by more than years and background. Although an adherent of the Liberal party, Howe's father was known as a high Tory, and Howe's personal inclinations were conservative. Tupper belonged to the Conservative party but, as early biographers pointed out, he was always a Conservative, never a Tory.[3] And in personality they were poles apart. Howe was a writer, a poet, an orator, a brilliant wit, who swayed his constituents with his silver tongue and pointed pen. He liked to please and enjoyed the accolades of the crowds. Tupper was a powerful, forceful pragmatist, who, having set his goals, pursued them relentlessly, never swaying from his principles or his vision. He had inherited his father's amazing memory as well as his drive and dogged determination. His skills as a speaker were based on his memory, his clarity of thought and his reputation as a fighter. When he had decided on a particular course of action he would allow nothing to get in his way. He not only liked to win, he assumed he would win.

Both men had strong feelings for Nova Scotia, but differing visions. Howe looked inward. He had a passionate attachment to the little colony of his birth, and he spoke and wrote about its virtues at every opportunity. Tupper looked outward, seeing Nova Scotia as part of a larger British presence in North America and in the world. Tupper admired the older Howe even as he opposed him. Howe disliked Tupper intensely, and it was part of his character to bear grudges.

In March of 1852, these men met on the political stage for the first time and Howe had won. But Tupper had made a considerable impression on the people of Amherst at this first skirmish, and the three years between then and the next election were not wasted. Frances made it clear she was not happy with the prospect of her husband in politics despite or perhaps because of her family familiarity with the political life; but she was impressed when she heard her husband making speeches and from that time was always an unreserved supporter of his political career. As a physician he was in daily contact with the people of the county, and whenever he could he made use of the opportunity to discuss politics. By the time the election was called he was assured of the nomination. The young doctor from Amherst defeated the established politician, writer and orator from Halifax. Conservatives were soundly defeated in other parts of the province, but the party took heart in the victory of the self-confident young physician who represented the future in Nova Scotia. On that campaign Tupper was already labelled "The Fighting Doctor." When Howe returned to Halifax and was asked about the young doctor who had unseated him, he responded that Nova Scotians would one day see that he had been unseated by "the leader of the Conservative Party." Howe was astute enough to recognize the potential of his young foe and clearly expected Tupper to step to the front of the party, a prophecy immediately fulfilled.

When the Conservative Premier, James Johnstone, called his party members together, he asked for young Tupper's opinions on party policy. Tupper made it clear that he believed the party was in error on two major policies. The first was the prevalent negative attitude towards Roman Catholics.[4] Tupper said that he believed there should be equal rights for all regardless of race or creed and that this policy should be boldly proclaimed. This was a wildly radical idea in the Nova Scotia of 1855, and most of the others present were shocked and disturbed by Tupper's recommendation.[5] Johnstone, however, said that he believed there might be some truth in what the young man proposed, both as to the Conservative policy of equal rights and Tupper's second recommendation, that the Conservative Party should drop all hostility to the railway policy of the government. Tupper had a vision of the future of the colony, and railroads were important in that vision.

Johnstone would remain Premier but he asked those present to recognize Charles Tupper as the new leader of the Conservative Party, and charged Tupper with implementing changes as he saw fit.

Dr. Charles Tupper, the young physician from Amherst, had begun his second career.

Chapter 4 – Notes

1. Saunders, E.M.; *The Life and Letters of the Right Hon. Sir Charles Tupper Bart. K.C.M.G.*; Cassell and Company, Ltd.. London. 1916. Vol. 1, page 39.

2. Grant, William Lawson; *The Tribune of Nova Scotia*. From *Chronicles of Canada*, in thirty-two volumes edited by George M. Wrong and H.H. Langton, Part VII The Struggle for Political Freedom. Glasgow, Brook and Company. Toronto. 1915. p. 153.

3. The allegiance of Tupper's family to the Conservative Party had been strengthened by Howe's battle in print with the conservative Baptists of Nova Scotia, which took place during Charles Tupper's days in Edinburgh.

4. This attitude was not only Conservative policy. Joseph Howe was a leader in what Sir Nicholas Meagher called "The Anti-Catholic Warfare". (*Howe and the Catholics*, also titled *The Religious Warfare in Nova Scotia*, by Sir Nicholas H. Meagher, published in Halifax, January, 1927.)

5. Longley (see ref. 1 chap. 3) suggests that Tupper's support of the rights of Catholics had an element of opportunism as well as principle, as Howe had always had a strong level of support from the Catholic community, but was losing it due to his support for the British war in the Crimean peninsula, and his attempt to raise soldiers in the United States for Britain (an illegal act until it was sanctioned by Howe who paid the recruits to come to Halifax to join), a cause not supported by the Catholics, especially the Irish in Halifax. The resulting confrontations for Howe with the angry Catholics made him appear, and later become, anti-Catholic. On the other hand, Sir Nicholas Meagher, a Catholic himself, writes that Howe was always anti-Catholic, so perhaps this incident simply made it evident.

Longley's view of the anti-Catholic debates of Howe and the Catholic support of Tupper, are hard to accept, in Meagher's opinion, as Longley distorts facts and was known to make up anti-Tupper stories during his career. After Tupper's death, the Tupper sons were upset that Longley planned a biography of Sir Charles, as he had admitted having spread lies about their father.

CHAPTER 5

Maritime Union

I n 1857 Tupper was asked to join a group of politicians from the North American British colonies to approach the British government for help in the building of the Intercolonial Railway. It was an exciting trip for Tupper. Transatlantic travel had much improved since his first visit to Great Britain, and Samuel Cunard's iron steamers could now cross the Atlantic in 9½ days. The government minister pleading their case would be the Colonial Secretary, Edward Bulwer-Lytton, (author of *The Last days of Pompeii*), whom Tupper admired.

Tupper had an audience with Queen Victoria and Prince Albert, spent time at Samuel Cunard's country home, and began a life-long friendship with Lord Carnarvon who was then Under-Secretary of State for the Colonies. He also briefly visited the famous and eccentric poet Martin Tupper, who was a distant relative.[1]

Unfortunately, even with Bulwer-Lytton's support, the group from the small colonies across the sea could not persuade the government to commit itself to the support of an intercolonial railway. It was disturbing to Tupper to bring a serious and important cause forward only to be refused like a small child waved off by a disinterested mother. The disappointment strengthened Tupper's belief, first in maritime union, and then in the union of all the British North American colonies into one autonomous nation, a force to be reckoned with. It was not his view that the colonies should be separated like the Americans, but that they should stand with Britian as an equal.

In one of his earliest speeches to the Legislature Tupper declared his political credo as supporting whatever he thought was best for the province, regardless of political doctrine.

I did not come here to play the game of follow my leader. I did not come here the representative of any particular party, bound to vote contrary to my own convictions, but to perform honestly and fearlessly to the best of my ability, my duty to my country. In the past I have seen measures, which lie at the root of all our prosperity and freedom, burked because they emanated from the leader of the Opposition; nor have the measures of the Government always received a dispassionate hearing from the Opposition. Whenever the measures of the Government commend themselves to my judgment, I shall not hesitate to support them.

In 1856 Howe had regained a seat in the house through a by-election. He continued his anti-Catholic rhetoric even as the Liberal government, under William Young, fell, giving the Conservatives a short tenure. Young and his colleagues recognizing that it was crucial to defeat the increasingly powerful Tupper in the election of 1859, put a lot of energy, money and patronage into the effort. Although the Liberals won by a narrow margin, they were not able to stop Tupper, who was re-elected. Howe became Premier, but his term was hampered by religious wrangling and constant attacks from Tupper, who daily led the opposition assault.

Despite his political involvement Tupper continued to practise medicine. When he was appointed Provincial Secretary he moved to Halifax with his family, which now included Sophie, born in 1858. The Amherst practice and the pharmacy were taken over by his younger brother, Dr. Nathan Tupper, who had also been his partner. Very soon he had a lucrative medical practice in Halifax and was appointed City Medical Officer. At the same time he became editor of *The British Colonist*, a Conservative newspaper published three times a week in Halifax, which provided him and his party with an excellent mouthpiece for Conservative comment.

There are numerous stories about adoring patients and dramatic successes at the hands of the young doctor practising in

Halifax. Many had grown taller with the years to enlarge the myth. One, as told by his sons, bears repeating.[2]

Mrs. Delaney was seriously ill and her doctors were uncertain what to do. They advised Mr. Delaney to call Tupper to ask him to visit. Mr. Delaney wasn't happy about the suggestion as he was an acknowledged political foe of Tupper. Finally, he relented and Tupper arrived; he sat up all night with Mrs. Delaney giving her champagne every half hour until she began to show signs of recovery. Tupper refused any fee. In the coming election Delaney still voted against him, but afterwards became a loyal supporter.

Dalhousie College

In 1862 an effort was made to enact the incorporation of Dalhousie College. Charles Tupper, William Young, Joseph Howe and S.L. Shannon were named the first provisional governors of the college. As a graduate of Edinburgh, and despite his father being a Baptist minister, Tupper was a strong supporter of the idea of a non-sectarian university. Nova Scotia already had several colleges, all connected with various Christian denominations. Scottish presbyterians had lobbied for a university like Edinburgh, which was open to all, regardless of religion; but the sectarian colleges objected strongly, arguing that this would give government sanction and money to a college which would be, to all intents and purposes, a Presbyterian college.

One of the strongest objectors was Acadia, the Baptist college in Wolfville, which had grown from Tupper's other Alma Mater, Horton Academy.[3] Part of its responsibility was to train young men for the Baptist ministry. Tupper's father was among those who had founded the college, and the Reverend Mr. Tupper openly opposed government support of Dalhousie.

The Act to incorporate Dalhousie's Board of Government was submitted to the Legislature by Howe, the Liberal leader, and was passed. The other Nova Scotia colleges objected strongly to its passage. Avard Longley, a Conservative, a Baptist and a friend of Acadia College, moved a resolution to rescind the Act, and intimated that opposition to the Act would continue until the colleges had achieved their objective. Tupper was in a difficult position, or perhaps we should say a position others might have found difficult. Generally, the Baptists supported his party. His own beloved father had signed the petitions that led to Longley's resolution to stop government support of Dalhousie. But that wasn't the way Tupper operated. As soon as Longley had finished speaking, Tupper sprang to his feet and spoke forcefully and eloquently in favour of the original Act, denouncing the attempts to have it set aside. He concluded:

> Sir, the honourable member for Annapolis has intimated that this agitation against Dalhousie College will continue until its walls are razed to its foundations and that those who endeavour to sustain it will be buried beneath their ruins. Let me tell him, sir, that, attached as I am to the great party with which I am connected, possessing, as I may confess I do, some fondness for the political life, I would infinitely prefer the fate which he threatens to the highest post my country can offer, if it must be purchased by an act so unpatriotic, so unjust as the resolution which he has moved would involve. [4]

Tupper's argument won the day. The resolution to rescind the Act of Incorporation for Dalhousie was defeated, with even Mr Johnstone voting against the negative resolution. Tupper was openly attacked by many, including the Reverend Dr. Cramp, President of Acadia College, but none of this seemed to bother him. In June of that year, when he was then Premier of Nova Scotia, he attended the anniversary exercises at Acadia, and the Alumni Dinner which followed, where he was unceremoniously accorded a seat at the end of the table. A friend commented on this to him, to which Tupper replied confidently, "Wherever the MacGregor sits, is the head of the table." At the end of the dinner a number of those present were invited to speak, but not Tupper. Never one to be ignored, Tupper surprised everyone by rising to speak anyway, and gave an impassioned speech in favour of the Act to incorporate Dalhousie, questioning the judgment of those who opposed the Act. He continued his support of Dalhousie as the years went on, and later introduced a resolution to found a Medical School at Dalhousie based on the Edinburgh model.

Despite his habit of barrelling through in defiance of popular opinion, always dangerous for a politician, Tupper and his party were growing in popularity. In May of 1863 Nova Scotia had yet another general election which was dominated by Dr. Charles

Tupper. His rivals, Joseph Howe and the Liberals, went down to a crushing defeat and William Johnstone became premier. Tupper still had a large and lucrative medical practice in Halifax which he said he could not afford to give up, so he formed a partnership with a Dr. Wickwire. It should have been a very happy time for Tupper, but it was marred by the death of his five year old daughter, Sophie, in a diphtheria epidemic that spread through the province in August, the first time the deadly disease had swept through Nova Scotia.

Although Johnstone was titular head of the government, it was obvious that Tupper was the true leader. It was to no one's surprise that in 1864, Johnstone was given a seat on the Bench, and Dr. Charles Tupper became Premier of Nova Scotia. He was 43 years old.

The Asylum for the Poor, and the Provincial Hospital

His increasing responsibilities did not prevent Tupper from practising medicine or from retaining his position as City Medical Officer. His years at Edinburgh had taught him a great deal about the relationship between poverty and illness, a subject which had been addressed in particular by his professor, William Pulteney Alison. A general hospital, the Provincial Hospital, had been built in Halifax but was not in use. On the other hand, the Asylum for the Poor, on Spring Garden Road, was crowded with over three hundred inmates. When illness occurred in the asylum, as it often did, it spread like wildfire among both inmates and staff. The sick in the Asylum for the Poor were not sent to the almost empty Provincial Hospital, but attempts were made to treat them at the asylum itself. Tupper's report to the City's Governing Board decried the situation.

> I cannot consistently, with what I consider to be my duty to the Board, close this report without making some suggestions which have forced themselves upon my mind in connection with the public health. The humane and enlightened treatment of poverty and disease is regarded as a matter of the highest importance in all well regulated communities. I do not think the treatment of either can be considered satisfactory in this city until a well-appointed hospital is put into operation. At the present, the Asylum for the Poor is crowded indiscriminately with those who simply require food and clothing, and those

who are suffering from the various forms of disease. A large portion of the three hundred inmates of that establishment are undoubtedly subjects for hospital treatment, and their removal to a purely medical institution could not but be attended with highly beneficial results to themselves and to those left behind, whose only misfortunes are their poverty and helplessness.

Tupper had a striking example to prove his point.

The treatment of contagious diseases under the present system is still more unsatisfactory. During the past summer no less than ten persons, including the Matron and principal Nurse, were lying at one time, in all stages of fever, in a small imperfectly ventilated building. The fever had assumed a highly contagious character, rendering it difficult to obtain suitable nurses. It is impossible that disease can be treated with success or satisfaction under such circumstances.

Tupper went on to argue that such a miserable state of affairs did not have to continue in the city of Halifax.

A large hospital has been erected in a suitable locality, medical men, well qualified to discharge the professional duties, can be obtained without difficulty, and the money required to sustain such an institution is now being expended without producing satisfactory results. Two thousand pounds are annually voted by the Legislature to the Poor's Asylum, about fifteen hundred pounds more are provided from civic funds in addition to a large sum annually expended in the treatment of contagious diseases; and two salaried medical officers are employed, one for the Poor's Asylum and the other for the fever hospital.

He concluded:

We are of the opinion that what we have stated proves in contestably the unfitness of the Poor's Asylum for Hospital purposes.

Not all of Tupper's medical colleagues agreed. As it happened, one of his best friends, William Almon, was the Medical Officer at the Asylum for the Poor. Following the presentation of the report Dr. Almon met Tupper on the street, and protested angrily that the report criticizing the care in the Asylum was unacceptable, and because of it their friendship was over. Tupper replied that he would regret losing Almon's friendship, but he would not change a report which he believed to be for the good of the people for whom he was responsible. Almon's anger didn't last, and shortly after their argument, he nominated Tupper as President of the Nova Scotia Medical Society, a post he accepted in 1863.

The Provincial Legislature agreed with Tupper's arguments. During the 1864 session legislation was passed providing both for the support of the hospital and the building of a new Poor House on the western part of the hospital grounds. There was some opposition to this by the City of Halifax, which owned the property as common land, known as the South Commons, but the Poor House was eventually built and served as a home for the indigent for nearly one hundred years.[5]

The Provincial and City Hospital began to thrive. Several appointments were made to the medical staff. Daniel MacNeill Parker and William Almon were named consulting physician and surgeon. Rufus Black, A.J. Cowie, W.H. Davies and A. Hattie were appointed attending physicians, and Charles Tupper, Edward Jennings, W.B. Slayter and John Ternan were named attending surgeons. There was also a management committee with Rufus Black as chair and Charles Twining, Henry Prior and Daniel MacNeill Parker as members. In 1867 the hospital admitted 227 patients.

Free Education

The 1864 session of the Nova Scotia Legislature also saw the introduction of another program of great importance. Tupper introduced the Education Act which provided education for all Nova Scotia children, administered by the government and financed by direct taxation.

Tupper was not the first to espouse free education for all children. Joseph Howe spoke often of the need for such a system. However, he also knew that the system would have to be financed by direct taxation and to introduce such a measure would mean his and his government's defeat. In a speech in the House of Assembly in 1855, Howe seemed to predict the arrival of a Tupper to carry such a politically dangerous program to success. Howe backed off from any hint that he might carry it forward. He said that the measure would some day be carried through but "Providence had first to catch an enthusiast, young enough to carry this question to its final conclusion . . . to agitate the masses and go through the country beating the rough clods of the valley and getting something like vitality to spring up in the soil." The man might not be in the house now, he said, but sure he was that such a man would be here before many years and that he would "with a free and fearless heart rouse up the spirit of the people and sweep away the obstructions now remaining in the path of the general education of the people."[6]

Howe was right. Just three months later young Dr. Tupper unseated him in Cumberland. When he became Premier Tupper, free general education was first on his list of things he must do. His government would institute a system of free schools supported by sectional taxation, aided by provincial and county grants. Despite the dangers to a government which attempted to institute a measure that would increase taxes, he saw it as the right thing to do, and he would do it.

Of course, education had not been totally neglected in Nova Scotia. Kings College, Horton Academy and Acadia College, Arichat College (which became St. Francis Xavier College), Pictou Academy and the Normal School at Truro were all admirable developing institutions. There were also voluntary common schools. To open a school, a teacher had to search the area for prospective students. A county board of school commissioners would provide a school house and would license the teacher. Tupper had attended one of these schools, taught by Jonathon McCully. This system was patchy at best, totally inadequate at worst and, as always, children of the poor suffered most.

Tupper and other advocates of a free school system knew that it had to be done. They also knew that it would be bitterly opposed by most of the people and by many of their political colleagues. Longley, one of Tupper's early biographers, comments that the average country member of the legislature was one "whose ideas generally do not reach very far beyond the question of re-election." He comments further, "The ordinary member of a provincial Assembly is not heroic, nor has he any predilections in the direction of reform or even change. He instinctively dislikes whatever is disturbing."[7] With Tupper at the helm, there would be reform, there would be change, and it would be disturbing.

Added to the challenge of convincing the electorate they should accept an increase in taxes, Tupper had decided that free education must be non-sectarian. Until then, Tupper's advocacy of freedom and equality for all citizens had made him, a Baptist, a champion of Nova Scotia Catholics. But now, with his concept of free education, the Catholics would find themselves in the position of either closing the Catholic schools, or financing their own schools and at the same time paying direct taxation to support the non-sectarian common schools. And the rules which Tupper proposed were not easy. Every teacher would be required to receive his or her licence from a central Council of Public Instruction. Members of religious orders who wished to teach would have to pass the same examinations as other teachers. Worse in the eyes of the Catholics, no religious education would be allowed in the schools, and the textbooks would be provided by the same Council of Public Instruction. Despite pressure, Tupper refused to retreat from any of these proposals.

The first part of the proposal, introduced in 1864, merely set up the Council and defined the duties and responsibilities of the county trustees. It left the financing of the schools to each school section. But in the 1865 session Tupper introduced the dreaded direct taxation amendment. There was much alarm, both within and outside the House. To weaken the initiative, a separate schools amendment was introduced, which would have allowed a separate school in any area if a certain number of taxpayers requested it. Tupper would have none of this. He said:

> "In the existing condition of things in this country, any system
> of common school education that involved the introduction
> of separate schools and prevented all denominations of
> Christians into which our community is divided from cooperat-
> ing with each other - which would not allow all children,
> irrespective of sect, to sit side by side, and learn those
> branches of education which are taught in the common and
> superior schools in this country - struck at the very foundation
> of our school system."[8]

The amendment to modify the proposal was defeated.[9] Longley says that the Education Act was "the most useful and beneficial measure passed by the Legislature since Responsible

Government was introduced. Its influence upon the intellectual life and moral tone of the Province was far-reaching. It was the first system of free non-sectarian schools adopted in any Province of British North America."[10]

An Epidemic of Cholera

In April 1866, a cholera epidemic occurred in the port of Halifax, and Tupper, as the City Medical Officer, Premier of the province and provincial secretary, was immediately notified of the outbreak by Dr. John Slayter, a health officer.

Major cholera epidemics were first noted in India in 1817, and outbreaks occurred in many parts of the world over the next four decades due to expanding travel, with epidemics in Quebec and Halifax in the 1830s and in Saint John, New Brunswick, in 1854 where 1600 people died. Halifax was threatened again in 1866 when the immigrant steamship *England*, bound for New York with 1207 passengers, requested permission to enter the harbour. A case of cholera had occurred on board and by the time the ship approached Halifax there were 160 ill and 46 dead, with fresh cases each day. A Halifax physician, Dr. John Garvie, bravely offered to sail with the ship back to New York, but the ship's agents, Cunard Company, indicated the crew were not fit to continue and asked permission to enter the port. Dr. Slayter had the ship anchor off Hangman's Beach on McNab's Island (so named because in the previous century mutineers were left hanging in sight of passing ships as a warning to their crews). Slayter's action kept the infection away from the city, and after notifying Dr. Tupper he joined the ship in quarantine to take charge of the epidemic and to treat the sick.

Slayter moved the healthy passengers ashore on McNab's Island, and 400 sick to HMS *Pyramus*, a naval hulk used in the harbour as a hospital ship. Slayter's call for medical help was responded to by Dr. Charles Gossip, Dr. John Garvie and his younger brother, Frank Garvie, who was a medical student at Harvard. Dr. W.N. Wickwire was assigned to inspect other ships entering the harbour. Police patrolled the waters to prevent any contact with locals. The death toll was rising rapidly and it was an eerie sight to see the longboats filled with bodies trailing from the stern of both ships with others anchored off the beach.

Archbishop Connelly, a friend of Tupper's, rowed out to McNab's Island to assess the accommodation for the passengers. On his appeal, Father MacIssac and three recently arrived Sisters of Charity from New York, Mary Vincent Power, Mary Claire Connelly and Mary Alphonse Doucet, went to the island to assist with the sick.

Although Slayter had things quickly in hand, Tupper issued directives to keep the epidemic confined and the passengers limited to one end of the island, with the dead buried quickly on a narrow neck of land at the southern tip.

Because no one would assist the doctors, they had to row as many as 30 coffins from Hangman's Beach to Thrum Cap, carry the coffins 200 yards inland and dig the graves out of the cold ground. The doctors toiled without rest, removing each newly dead body, and even swabbing down the decks of the *Pyramus* where so many were dying.

To add to their trouble, as Slayter's message to Tupper related, they had difficulty in maintaining control on the island because of the animosity between the German and the Irish passengers, each blaming the other for having brought the disease on board. Also, those without friends or protectors were in danger from dying of starvation. They were mostly women and children, who were excluded from the food stores and even from the tents and had to seek refuge in the woods. April in Nova Scotia can be bitter, and these souls were in danger of dying of exposure and cold. Slayter said the police were "as helpful as a fifth wheel on a coach," spending their time on their schooner when they were supposed to be patrolling the island and waters.

Tupper feared the circumstances on the island might drive some to try to escape, raising the danger of spreading the disease; in fact, some did make it to the mainland. A few passengers were sighted outside Halifax, and one died of cholera some time later in Portland, Maine. The military was called in to keep the passengers confined to the southern aspects of the island. Not all the threats to public safety were easy to contain. One of four bodies, weighted and sunk into the harbour, floated to the surface and was hit by a fishing boat, which raised fears in the town.

Although the cause of cholera (vibrio cholerae) was not known and the contagionists and the non-contagionists each argued their side of the case, it was recognized that quarantine and sanitary measures were the only helpful ways to control an epidemic. Tupper believed the disease was spread by contagion and ordered everything associated with the cases to be burned. In his memoirs [11] he told of an incident which he believed confirmed his theory. He wrote:

> One Sunday morning a poor man, living in a small isolated house near the shore on the outskirts of Halifax, asked me to visit his child. The moment I saw the little girl it was evident that it was the dread disease. I called a policeman and told him not to allow anyone to enter or leave the house until I returned, then drove straight to the hospital, where I arranged for a room to be completely isolated. I then took the horse out of my wagon and put it in the ambulance, drove back to the house, took the sick child, with her father and mother, into the ambulance, and placed them in the isolated part of the hospital. As soon as I saw the child I asked the mother if she had used anything that had washed ashore from the ship *England*, which was anchored about a mile distant. She said she had not. The child and mother died, and the father, who was attacked, recovered. The mother before her death confessed that she found a piece of fine canvas on the shore, and made a petticoat for the little girl. I had the house and all it contained burned the next day. No other case occurred in Halifax. No more conclusive evidence has ever been given of the contagiousness of Asiatic cholera.

Tupper had indicated at the outset of the epidemic that he needed a full report from Slayter, but Slayter was so busy with other matters that he suggested a group of physicians be asked to formulate questions and he would provide answers that would constitute a report. He showed further impatience with the requests from the Lieutenant-Governor for twice daily telegrams, responding that the work they were doing on the island was a necessity but that news for the town was a luxury. When pressed for mortality figures by Dr. Prior he angrily suggested that he come to the island to see for himself, adding that doctors are "death-proof." Sadly, Dr. Slayter wasn't. A message to Tupper from the ship's agent on the 17th of April, eight days after the ship entered port, stated, "Dr. Slayter died at a quarter to ten o'clock this morning. Send a lead coffin from Halifax at once."

Dr. Slayter was the last case of cholera to occur, and the next day, while he was being buried on the island, the SS *England*, having completed the quarantine procedures, slipped out of the harbour bound for New York.

Maritime Union

Canadians recognize that Tupper was one of the Fathers of Confederation since he was present at the Charlottetown Conference of 1864 as a representative of Nova Scotia. It is not widely recognized, however, that the conference which led to Canada's confederation was originally called by Tupper to discuss maritime union.

The talk of confederation had been in the air for years. Francis Nicholson and Thomas Pownall before the American Revolutionary War, Chief Justice Sewell in 1814 and Lord Durham in his report, all favoured a union of the British colonies. But it was the government of Nova Scotia which began legislative discussion of union in 1854, and it was Charles Tupper, speaking at the opening of the Mechanics' Institute in Saint John, New Brunswick, in 1860, who revived the idea in a lecture, "The Political Condition of British North America." It was an eloquent, thoughtful talk, which has been called "one of the most remarkable of his career."[12]

He was unhappy with the British Government's treatment of the colonies, something which he had experienced first-hand on his visit to England in support of the Intercolonial Railway. He said, "Our position is ever one of uncertainty. We have no constitution but the dicta of the ever-changing occupants of Downing Street." Referring to the British method of government, he asked, "Was it such as to meet our material progress and satisfy the natural and laudable ambition of free and intelligent minds?"

"We are," he continued, "without name or nationality - comparatively destitute of influence and of the means of occupying the position to which we may justly aspire." He spoke angrily of New Brunswick land and maritime fishing rights given to the United States, with no discussion with the colonists, and without granting "adequate consideration for a sacrifice so immense." He spoke of British North America with pride, and looked forward to that day when British North America would include not only the Maritime Provinces, but also Upper and Lower Canada, "the great Red River and Saskatchewan country . . . and British Columbia."

Tupper saw the union of the maritime colonies, Nova Scotia, New Brunswick, Prince Edward Island and possibly Newfoundland as the first step towards this greater union. In 1864 he proposed to the legislature a resolution authorizing the government to contact the other maritime colonies with a view to organizing a conference to discuss union. The resolution passed easily and Tupper immediately contacted the other provinces whose leaders agreed to a conference to be held in Charlottetown in September.

Tupper decided that, along with himself, the delegates should include William Henry, the Attorney-General of the time, and the Hon. Robert Dickey of Amherst, representing the party in power; the Hon. A.G. Archibald and Joseph Howe representing the opposition Liberals. Howe was out of the government by this time, but Tupper respected his ability and recognized his standing among Liberals in Nova Scotia, and among Nova Scotians in general. Howe, however, wrote that he was too busy to attend, but that he wished the conference well, and would give his support to any proposal that he thought fair. Tupper appointed Jonathon McCully in his place.

It soon became obvious that maritime union would not succeed at this time. Prince Edward Island was the main hold-out, insisting that it would only discuss union if it was agreed that the capital would be Charlottetown. However, the Maritimers had invited some visitors to their conference in the persons of seven representatives of Canada, as Ontario and Quebec were then called. John A. Macdonald, George Brown, George Etienne Cartier, Alexander Galt, William McDougall, D'Arcy McGee, Alexander Campbell and Hector Langevin joined the maritime representatives at Charlottetown to discuss the case for the union of the colonies. At a gala banquet in Charlottetown, Tupper addressed the assembled guests:

> I feel assured that all will endorse the sentiment that it is our
> duty and interest to cement the colonies together by every
> tie that can add to their greatness. A union of the North
> American provinces would elevate their position, consolidate
> their influence and advance their interests; and, at the same
> time, continue their fealty to their mother country and their
> Queen, which fealty is the glory of us all. The British-American
> statesman who does not feel it is his duty to do all in his
> power to unite politically, socially and commercially the

British provinces is unworthy of his position and is unequal to the task submitted to him.

It was a strong call to union and one which continued as the representatives from Canada continued their tour through the Maritimes.

From a historical point of view, one of the most important events of the conference was the meeting of Dr. Tupper from Nova Scotia and John A. Macdonald from Canada. They became strong friends and powerful allies. Macdonald knew what he wanted to do and he recognized immediately that Tupper had the strength, persistence and the dogged determination to act. Tupper "declared openly and unequivocally what he proposed to do and depended upon main force to remove difficulties and secure success."[13]

The colonies' representatives met again in October, this time in Quebec. Once a proposal for confederation had been formulated the arguments and fighting began. In Canada, the tariff was high and the public debt large. There had been much in-fighting between the quarrelling factions and legislation was often deadlocked. In the maritime colonies of Nova Scotia, New Brunswick and Prince Edward Island, on the other hand, the public debt was low and revenues were always on the increase. Trade was good and the colonies were prosperous. Maritimers in general, especially the bankers and wealthy merchants, saw no reason to change the status quo. The government of Canada did nothing to help the cause when it proposed a budget with greatly increased expenditure and, worst of all, made a proposal to issue fishing licences to foreign countries. Maritimers saw that proposal as a sacrifice of the lucrative maritime fishery; in fact, this is considered by many to be a factor in the collapse of the maritime fishery today, 120 years later.

In New Brunswick, Tilley faced a general election and was defeated. Prince Edward Island and Newfoundland remained solidly against Union. Anti-union sentiment was strong in Nova Scotia, but Tupper was strong too, having enlisted an impressive array of leaders from both parties supporting the move to unite. He called a meeting in Halifax at which prominent supporters of union spoke. But the anti-union movement was growing, and a few days later the anti-unionists held a meeting in the same hall. Among others on the platform was Joseph Howe. He didn't speak, but before long anonymous editorials against confederation – "The Botheration Scheme" – began to appear in the anti-unionist *Morning Chronicle*, editorials that bore the unmistakable touch of Joseph Howe. The final, major struggle between the "fighting doctor" from Amherst and the seasoned orator from Halifax had begun.

In the legislature Tupper brought forward a motion to reconsider maritime union now that the situation in New Brunswick made the larger union improbable, but the British government wasn't enthusiastic about this proposal. William Miller, a young independent politician, made an eloquent speech in favour of the larger union, recommending that delegates be appointed whose role it would be to negotiate a better deal for Nova Scotia within the union. Since Miller had previously opposed union, his speech came as a surprise to everyone, even to Tupper. But Tupper knew an opening when we saw one, and on the 10th of April 1866 he proposed a union resolution. "Tupper never made pretence of nice scruples; to reach the goal was his supreme object."[14] He twisted an arm here, made an offer of patronage there, and at 2:00 a.m. on 18 April 1867 the vote was taken. It was 31 to 19 in favour of Tupper's resolution for union. Nova Scotia would be part of the union, part of British North America, part of Canada.

Chapter 5 – Notes

1. Martin Tupper (1810-1889) became internationally known for his poetry in a Victorian age that enjoyed syrupy and emotional poems. Truly a flash in the pan, he went from being widely idolized to being a joke in a very few years.

2. Letter written by William Tupper to his brother Charles Hibbert Tupper, asking him to include the story of Mrs. Delaney in a memoir of his father. Charles Hibbert Tupper's papers in the Provincial Archives of Nova Scotia. p. 3308.

3. Other Nova Scotia Colleges were the Anglican King's College and the Catholic Saint Mary's College, both in Halifax and Saint Francis Xavier, which began in Arichat and then moved to Antigonish.

4. Longley, J.W.; *Sir Charles Tupper*. Toronto. Makers of Canada (Morang) Ltd. 1916: (Parkman Edition) p. 47.

5. It was eventually demolished in the 1960s as Mrs Killam did not want such a building beside the Izaak Walton Killam Hospital for Children, to which she had substantially contributed in her husband's name. A new chronic care hospital was built, the Abbey Lane Hospital, on the grounds of the Camp Hill Hospital, but it was ill-designed as the city did not make it clear whether this was to be a home for indigents or a mental hospital. A role and mission was later defined and redefined as the hospital changed with the changing needs; at present it houses an acute mental hospital, and the University Departments of Family Medicine and Psychiatry. The site of the original Poor Asylum is now occupied by the new Grace Maternity Hospital.

6. Longley, J.W.; *Sir Charles Tupper*. Toronto. Makers of Canada (Morang) Ltd. 1916: (Parkman Edition) p. 31.

7. Ibid p. 33.

8. Ibid p. 39.

9. After the passage of the Act, Tupper and the Archbishop were able to effect a compromise which Catholics, other denominations and the government could live with. The schools built by the church were rented to the government, which then administered them from the general fund. Catholic teachers were trained and licensed by the Council, but appointed by the Catholic members of the School Board. Religious instruction was given after school hours in the rectory.

10. Longley, p. 40.

11. *The Life and Letters of the Rt. Hon. Sir Charles Tupper, Bart. K.C.M.G.*, Vol.1; Edited by E.M. Saunders D.D., London. Cassell & Company Ltd., 1916; Vol. 2, p. 127-128.

12. Longley, p. 54.

13. Longley, p. 65.

14.Longley, p. 85.

The birthplace of Sir Charles Tupper in Amherst, which was demolished earlier
in this century. *Carl W. Pridham photo.*

The Town of Amherst, Nova Scotia, where Charles Tupper was born.
From the Canadian Illustrated News, December 9, 1876.

Town of Wolfville, Nova Scotia, where Tupper entered Horton Academy.
Canadian Illustrated News, March 16, 1872.

i

Tupper's father, the Reverend Charles Tupper, a leader in the Baptist clergy and temperance movement of the Maritimes. From "Life and Letters", Vol. 1.

Tupper as a young man. From an oil painting by an unidentified artist, in "Life and Letters", Vol. 1.

Edinburgh professors, 1850. Front row: James Young Simpson (midwifery), Robert Jameson (natural history), William Pulteney Alison (medicine), Thomas Stewart Traill (medical jurisprudence); Back row: James Miller (surgery), John Hutton Balfour (medicine and botany), and John Hughes Bennett (institutes of medicine).

(Above.)
A young Frances Tupper with
daughter Emma. From "Life and Letters" Vol. 1.

(Right.)
The young professional Tupper,
an experienced physician, an
inexperienced politician.
From "Recollections of Sixty Years".

The drugstore started in Amherst by Dr. Charles Tupper and his brother
Dr. Nathan Tupper is shown on the corner, with a horse and wagon outside.
Courtesy Provincial Archives of Nova Scotia.

Tupper in 1864, Premier of Nova Scotia. From "Recollections of Sixty Years".

The representatives at the 1864 Charlottetown Conference. Tupper is seen third from the left in the back row. He initiated this conference to discuss Maritime Union but the idea was expanded to the concept of a wider confederation.

The Fathers of Confederation at the signing of the the resolutions that led to the British North America Act of 1867. Tupper is seen speaking on the right. The original painting by Robert Harris, first damaged in a fire in the Quebec Parliament Building, was later destroyed in the Parliament Building fire in 1916. It was repainted by Rex Wood in 1964, commissioned by the Confederation Life Insurance Company.

Sir John A. Macdonald.

The Macdonald orchestra, with Tupper playing the bass on the left.

Louis Riel was visited by Tupper in 1869.
Photo by Abraham Guay.

Joseph Howe.
Courtesy Provincial Archives of Nova Scotia.

vi

Dalhousie College on Grand Parade in Halifax. Dalhousie Medical School began in this building with one room for lectures and an attic room for dissection.
Courtesy Dalhousie University.

THE SYNDICATE'S CHRISTMAS TREE;
OR, THE TIME FOR GIVING THINGS AWAY.

Cartoon lampooning the CPR syndicate's deals.
From Canadian Illustrated News.

THE PACIFIC YOUNGSTER PACIFIED.

CHARLES.—"WELL, THEN, AND DID HIS BAD, BAD MACKENZIE MAKE A FOOLEY TOOLEY OF HIM, SO HE DID; BUT HE SHALL HAVE HIS ISLAND RAILWAY, SO HE SHALL; AND HE'LL ALWAYS VOTE FOR HIS SIR CHARLEY, SO HE SHALL!"

Cartoon showing Tupper's tendency to make whatever deals would build the CPR. From Canadian Illustrated News.

*Sir Charles Tupper in 1870, when he was in his third term as
President of the Canadian Medical Association.*
From "Recollections of Sixty Years". Photo by W. Notman, Montreal.

Sir Charles Tupper in 1881.
From "Recollections of Sixty Years".
Photo by Bradley and Rullofson, San Francisco.

Lady Tupper.
Photo by Topley, Ottawa.
From "Recollections of Sixty Years".

Dr. William Osler.

Sir Andrew Clark. Royal College
of Physicians, London.

Sir Charles Hibbert Tupper.

Sir Charles Tupper in 1896, as High Commissioner to London. A portrait presented by some of his London friends.
From "Life and Letters", Vol.2.

Lady Aberdeen, wife of the Governor General.

The Mount, Bexleyheath, outside London, where Tupper lived in his last years. The manor looked onto the first tee of a local golf course where he played until age 90. The only remaining buildings are the gardener's house, not visable behind the manor, and the circular brick garden gazebo on the left.

Tupper, the elder statesman.
Courtesy Audiovisual Services,
Dalhousie Medical School.

Senior statesman at 93.
From "Life and Letters", Vol.2.

The Funeral procession along Barrington St., Halifax, to St. Paul's Church. Later
Sir Charles Tupper was laid to rest in Fairview Cemetary beside Lady Tupper.
Courtesy Provincial Archives of Nova Scotia.

The plaque at Tupper's gravesite from the Government of Canada commemorating his role as a delegate to the intercolonial conferences in 1864 and 1867.

The grave of Charles Tupper is surrounded by granite stones marking his contribution to the Government of Canada.

The plaque at Tupper's gravesite from the Canadian Medical Association commemorating his role as its first president.

The bust of Sir Charles Tupper in the entrance of the Canadian Medical Association, and an identical one, gift of the CMA, in the foyer of the Sir Charles Tupper Medical Building at Dalhousie University.
Courtesy Audiovisual Services, Dalhousie Medical School.

The Sir Charles Tupper Medical Building at Dalhousie Medical School, dedicated on the 100th anniversary of Canadian Confederation in 1967 as Nova Scotia's Confederation project.
Courtesy Audiovisual Services, Dalhousie Medical School.

CHAPTER 6

Confederation

The delegates from the Canadian colonies met in the Westminster Palace Hotel in London where Tupper made the suggestion that John A. Macdonald should be the chairman. Tupper recognized that although he could take the concept through the hard-fought early stages, the move towards confederation now needed someone with a more diplomatic and persuasive approach; he felt Macdonald was "an extremely attractive personality and was unequalled as a tactician." They worked on the resolutions for twenty days and submitted them on 26 December 1866. With minor amendments they were passed by the Imperial Government on 9 March 1867.

Tupper returned home and gained agreement for union from Nova Scotia. The British North America (BNA) Act passed into effect on 1 July 1867. Lord Monck, the first Governor General, asked Macdonald to form the government. Confederation had been achieved and Tupper's vision of a grand union, now called Canada, was becoming a reality.

Meanwhile, the London conference was a signal to Howe and the anti-confederates to rise up. They sent a delegation to London to oppose and reverse the union. Howe spread pamphlets widely which insisted that union would be bad for the maritime colonies, urging instead a federation of the whole Empire with representation from Nova Scotia and New Brunswick. Tupper answered the arguments of Howe in a powerful and eloquent response, mustering all of his arguments from Howe's earlier public speeches and writings when he was a supporter of confederation. Howe would repeatedly have to answer to his own words.

When the Morning Star changed its policy on confederation by supporting Howe's arguments, Tupper met with the editors and demanded they publish his reply to Howe; he further insisted that if Howe did not respond, the newspaper must acknowledge its mistake. Tupper's answer to Howe was succinct and hardhitting. Howe did not respond and the newspaper carried through with its agreement and indicated it would again support confederation. Tupper then published a pamphlet in response to Howe, and once again Howe remained silent. There was little opposition when the BNA Act came to the vote. It is easy to see why John A. Macdonald would come to regard Tupper as his "enforcer".

At this point, when the government was to be formed, the other representatives (but not Tupper), were upset that Macdonald was awarded the KCB (Knight Commander of the Bath) by the Queen, while they each received the lesser award of CB (Companion of the Bath). A more serious disagreement developed over the distribution of portfolios to the representatives from Ontario and Quebec, designed to reflect their larger populations. When Macdonald concluded that agreement could not be reached on the formation of a new government, he decided in frustration to ask the Governor General to urge the Hon. George Brown to form the new government. Unhappy with this, Tupper went that evening to see the Hon. D'Arcy McGee and told him of his solution: if McGee would agree to join with him in resigning, there would be positions available to create the necessary balance of representation.

The next day Macdonald called a meeting in the Council Chamber to proclaim his failure and his decision to announce that he was giving up the challenge. Tupper then provided his planned solution of a simple rearrangement of representation of the many groups in the new ministries, made possible by Tupper himself stepping aside to allow another representative to take his place, and with McGee, who represented Irish Catholics, doing the same. Many of the representatives had come to the meeting that morning with their coats over their arms expecting to leave for home, but

Macdonald proclaimed, "Tupper has found a solution," and in less than fifteen minutes a cabinet was formed.

Having watched Tupper give up the opportunity to be a minister in the new confederation he fought so hard for, Macdonald was understandably concerned about what he would now choose – become a Governor or a Lieutenant-Governor? Tupper replied, "I would not take all the governorships rolled into one. I intend to run for a seat in the Dominion Parliament." And so he returned home to run for election as an ordinary citizen and member of his party.

The campaign was a bitter one, with Joseph Howe churning up more anti-confederation emotions. The two rivals met in debate at Truro. Tupper continued to chide Howe with his own previous arguments in favour of confederation and with his recent audiences with Queen Victoria. The Queen had indicated her congratulations to Tupper on his efforts to achieve confederation and had added, "I take the deepest interest in it, for I believe it will make them great and prosperous." Howe reminded the audience that Tupper had not been made a member of the new government. Tupper conceded in his speech that it was true that he was not a minister in the new government, but did not mention why. In another debate with Howe he was about to comment on an item in the newspaper when he realized he was unable to read the small print. He went on from memory but from then on he used reading glasses.

Howe had great effect with his speeches, proclaiming broadly that Nova Scotia had been sold into bondage. Tupper won the next election against Mr. Annand by a mere 94 votes, but the other supporters of Confederation, including Archibald who had been appointed to the federal cabinet, went down to defeat. Anti-unionists won every seat except Tupper's in the federal government and all but two in the provincial government (the two elections were held at the same time).

Macdonald asked Tupper if he would take Archibald's place as Secretary of State for the Provinces, but Tupper refused. Tupper was then offered the chairmanship of the Intercontinental Railway Commission at a salary of $5000 while retaining his seat in the House of Commons, but again he declined. In March, 1868, he wrote to Macdonald to explain his refusal, as he had earlier said he would consider the offer. On reflection he felt it would remove him further from the cause of confederation; he wanted Nova Scotians to come cordially into confederation and he could only work to that end "if untrammelled by such an office."

Although Tupper had his own reasons for refusing offices, as he felt they would lessen his ability to win the Confederation issue at home in Nova Scotia, he would always be loyal to John A., usually responding to any request to come to his aid. On one occasion when Macdonald wanted to delay discussion in the House so that a certain motion would not be reached in that sitting, he asked Tupper, famous for his ability to deliver long, logical, organized speeches with little preparation and without notes, to stall the House. "What do you wish me speak on?" Tupper asked. Looking at his list to see what would come up before the item to be delayed, Macdonald said "The motion of the Finance Minister respecting the rate of interest is before it – speak on that." Tupper replied, "Unfortunately, I am opposed to that measure." Sir John shrugged and said, "Well, speak against it, then." Tupper stood and spoke for over an hour, until signalled by Macdonald that it was no longer necessary to continue. He took his seat, but the issue he took on, which was previously supported by a majority of 30, went down to defeat by a majority of 8.[1]

Tupper had suggested at the Quebec Conference a method for forming the Senate by appointing current legislative councillors to the first seats to keep the balance between the two parties, and this was done.

Anticonfederation Movement

One might think that when the first of July celebrations of 1867 hailed the birth of the new Canada, that the anti-confederation arguments would be set aside. But Joseph Howe and many others were still hopeful of turning the process around. The anti-unionists in control of the legislature in Nova Scotia passed a motion to send an address to the Queen praying that union would be repealed. To counteract this movement Macdonald asked Tupper if he would go to England, taking Galt with him. Galt, however, refused to accompany Tupper, as he said the antagonism was so bitter between Tupper and Howe that nothing could come from this. Macdonald also wanted Tupper to raise two other issues in London: the refusal of the Americans to pay an increased licensing fee for fishing in

Canadian waters, and the need to secure a grant from the British government for £4,000,000 sterling towards the cost of the Intercolonial Railway.

The first person Tupper called upon when he arrived in London was Joseph Howe. Howe was not available, so Tupper left his card and awaited a response. Howe called and greeted him, "Well, I can't say I'm glad to see you, but we have to make the best of it." Tupper said the matter was indeed serious but frankness was required. Tupper continued, "I will not insult you by suggesting that you should fail to undertake the mission that brought you here. When you find out, however, that the Government and the Imperial Parliament are overwhelmingly against you, it is important for you to consider your next step."

Howe threatened to have his many supporters in every county refuse to pay taxes and defy the government to enforce confederation. Tupper replied that Howe had no power over taxation but if he acted in such a way, in a short time everyone would curse him as there would be no money for schools, roads or bridges. Tupper then said that although he would not exercise his power as Premier by calling in troops, he would see that the federal subsidy would be withheld, which would further embarrass Howe and his supporters. He reminded him that all the bishops, judges, clergy and "the best elements in the province" supported union.

Tupper showed Howe the letter he had sent to Macdonald declining the chairmanship of the Intercolonial Railway Board and any other portfolio until he had a "majority from Nova Scotia at my back." He pointed out that Howe had a majority at his back, and if he would join the federal cabinet and assist in the work of confederation he would be given control of all provincial patronage and would have in Tupper as strong a supporter as he had been an opponent.

Tupper said he "saw at once that Howe was staggered" by the offer of controlling so much patronage, and after two hours of frank discussion he knew Howe would eventually come around and said so that night in a letter to Macdonald. His argument had been clear and simple. Howe could not win; persistence would be regarded as mischief, bringing Howe and his party to ruin. On the other hand, if he would return to Nova Scotia and tell his supporters that they should give confederation a fair trial, the federal government would be willing to make concessions to Nova Scotia. Since Tupper had refused a seat in government, a Nova Scotia seat would be available for Howe.

Howe indicated that he still wanted to make a strong case against the union, but if it became clear that nothing was going to happen he would abide by whatever Nova Scotians decided. Howe had been impressed by Tupper's comments and offer and "said a good many civil things," but he was worried that if he agreed his supporters would abandon him. Tupper encouraged him by saying that between them, and together, they could rally three fourths of the wealth, education and influence in Nova Scotia, and Howe would be favoured by the Crown.

A few days later Tupper again wrote to Macdonald to indicate he had made significant headway with Howe. He noted with sadness the tragic assassination of D'Arcy McGee, who had agreed to step aside with Tupper to save the new government, and asked that the government provide every financial support for his family.[2] In his last speech, an hour before he died, McGee was defending Tupper from criticisms about his multiple appointments, and "spoke eloquently about your merits," said Macdonald.[3]

Tupper wrote to Macdonald that the British were gratified by his arrival in London, as "Howe and Company" were causing some anxiety by their talk to the politicians and the newspapers. He mentioned his disagreement with Macdonald's prior suggestion that he stay away from the newspapers, although he dutifully did so. He outlined the meeting with Howe, and the positions and rewards that had been suggested if Howe would join in support of the Government. He also noted, with some pride, he had heard from others that at a party a few nights later Howe had been speaking of Tupper in most complimentary terms.

The Duke of Buckingham invited Tupper to Stowe Park for the Easter holidays. This gave Tupper the opportunity to address the position of Canada with the USA on fisheries, the loan for the Intercolonial Railway and the need to turn back the anti-unionist movement. The Duke asked if there were any members of Parliament at Westminster he would like to meet to review the impending House of Commons discussion of Canadian confederation. Tupper said the only guests he personally would like to see invited were Mr. and Mrs. Joseph Howe.

He had another request of Buckingham. Recognizing the sensitivity in Quebec over the higher award to Sir John A. Macdonald than to Cartier and the other representatives, Tupper, Galt, and Tilley, he put in a good word to the Duke about Cartier and said he was as strong in Quebec as John A. was in Ontario, and warranted equal recognition by the Crown. Later discussions with the Queen indicated there would have to be a delay until a vacancy in the Order of Bath occurred, so Tupper suggested another solution, which was acted upon, to make Cartier a baronet to heal the wound felt in Quebec.

After three days at Stowe in pleasant discussion Tupper was convinced that Howe would come into line, and before he left he met with him to offer reassurance about Howe's concerns that his supporters would abandon him if he took this course. Writing to Macdonald, Tupper emphasized that he had assured Howe of a seat in cabinet and seats for Nova Scotia members on the Intercolonial Railway Board, plus "the most favorable consideration, financially and otherwise, for the province from your Government." The matter with Howe, if now managed judiciously by Macdonald, could be regarded as settled. Tupper also felt he had influenced the mind of the British Parliament, as well as the press and the public, about the importance of Canadian confederation "despite the extreme and general ignorance which prevails here [in England] regarding everything on the other side of the Atlantic."

On 20 June 1868 he again wrote to Sir John A. Macdonald to repeat what he had offered to Howe so there would be no waffling or backtracking on these commitments. Tupper told Macdonald he would step aside but remain loyal to Confederation and give it a chance. On the other hand, if Howe did not show loyalty once the agreement was made, Tupper growled, he would go across the province speaking to every group he could find, confident he could defeat Howe on the stages, stumps and soapboxes of every community. Howe would be given every consideration if cooperative; otherwise, Tupper would destroy him.

Tupper was invited to private dinners by those sympathetic to the Canadian union such as Sir Harry Verney, who would invite about 30 prominent gentlemen to dine each time. It was interesting dinner converation, as Sir Harry was the brother-in-law of Florence Nightingale, and he was able to talk to prominent British physicians.

One shared his love of travel in Canada, and was perhaps the first to do so coast to coast as an adventurous tourist. Dr. Walter Cheadle, author of *Northwest Passage by Land*, engaged him in a discussion of the treatment of Indians, and of the Hudson's Bay Company.

It remained for Howe to recognize the failure of his attempts to sway the British parliamentarians and the newspapers of the "error of confederation."

Sir John A. had instructed Tupper not to use the newspapers in fighting Howe, but Howe was making hay with the press and directly with the politicians. Although it was not a plan of Tupper to get around this order, an English MP provided the means. Sir Edward Watkins got permission from Tupper to reprint the Tupper speech from the previous year in which he answered Howe on the subject of union, using Howe's words when he was in favour of confederation. It was distributed to every member of both Houses and had a major effect in sealing Howe's defeat. Although there was serious concern by many in the British Government that Howe's argument was initially having some effect, especially since the union was not a permanent arrangement, the published Tupper speech did the trick. The House of Commons refused the appeal against confederation, voting it down 181 to 87.

Many of the arguments about the stability of the confederation of Canada, the appropriate representation of various factions, and issues of Quebec's status may today seem quite current. Tupper had also acted for the Government in matters regarding relations with the USA, particularly the fishing licences for Americans fishing in Canadian waters. He could report to Macdonald that he was successful in having the increased licence approved.

It was time to leave for home, but Macdonald said it was dangerous to leave Howe in London, so he should make sure he stayed until Howe was ready to leave. They sailed on the *City of York* on the 4th of July and landed in Halifax, but not without difficulty, as the ship went aground on a shoal off Sambro Head just outside Halifax Harbour. Tupper was washing and was thrown against the washbasin. He quickly changed from his nightshirt before going on deck, taking care to remove twelve heavy penny pieces from his pocket, money he had won from Howe at shuffleboard the evening before. (How ignominious to drown weighted down by winnings from Howe!) Fortunately the ship was able to reverse off the shoal without damaging the hull. As Tupper came down the gangway he was greeted by cheers, but Howe received even greater applause when he appeared. In the next weeks, however, Howe's supporters would gradually grow suspicious of his recommendations that there should be renewed discussions between the two sides, and that there would be concessions for the anti-confederates.

When Tupper returned to Nova Scotia he did not meet often with Howe as he did not wish to be seen by Howe's colleagues to be too intimate with their leader just at the time Tupper expected him to come over to the Conservative side. Tupper went to Ottawa to report to Macdonald and he implored him to come to Nova Scotia to meet with Howe. Macdonald arrived with an entourage of prominent men including Sir George Etienne Cartier and the Premier of Ontario, John Sandfield Macdonald. Howe admitted to Sir John A. Macdonald he would still move against confederation if he could see a way, but J. S. Macdonald's response was to repeat Tupper's clear argument that there was no possibility of success, and that the British Parliament had firmly ruled against any repeal. Howe continued to worry about the best way to deal with his supporters who had many serious misgivings. Macdonald said he would give him a private letter that he could reveal as he wished, encouraging supporters to come to the aid of Howe and others who had been won over to the government side. From that moment Howe, Macdonald and Tupper were allies. Macdonald later wrote to Tupper congratulating him on his success in all of this, saying, "Howe has not only abandoned the ship 'Repeal' but has burned the ship." He went on to say that although Howe had not directly said so, he would now undoubtedly like to be on better personal terms with Tupper.

At this time Howe was confined to his house with infection of his eyes. There was one more meeting with Tupper about Howe's plan to run for election in Hants County. Tupper was anxious to support him, but Howe was anxious of the effect Tupper's speaking would have on his chances on the hustings. A compromise was reached with Tupper keeping silent on the public stage while he circulated a letter to the Conservatives indicating why they should vote for Howe.

Tupper's friends feared that he would follow D'Arcy McGee

and fall to an assassin's bullet. They were aware that McGee had been killed just after delivering a speech in defense of Tupper. His father had written to him in April to say that although he was a man of undaunted courage he should not take unnecessary risks, should not go out at night or even in the day if it seemed obviously dangerous. Undoubtedly aware that that was not Tupper's style, his father then advised that he should "earnestly strive to be in a state of preparation for the termination of this short and precarious life."

Although many of Howe's supporters could not accept his turnaround, he was able to take some with him. The most important was John Thompson, who had also been an anti-confederate. He switched with Howe and would become a colleague of Tupper's in later years.

In a letter to Macdonald, Tupper indicated that if Howe were to be defeated in Hants County he would step down and give Howe his seat. Howe was bitterly attacked by his friends and, to make matters worse, developed a severe inflammation of his bowels. When Tupper visited him he was shocked by his appearance, finding him "broken down" and very depressed. Tupper told him he was confident of his election, but if Howe lost, he would resign and give Howe his seat. Howe was touched by this offer but said he could never accept. The generous gesture was unnecessary as Howe was elected by a majority almost as large as when he ran as an anti-confederation candidate. Many of Howe's supporters now voted against him, but Tupper was pleased that he had been able to swing an equal number in support of Howe. In his journal Tupper noted that Howe took his seat in Ottawa, but as a broken man and a wreck of his former self. Tupper took no pleasure in seeing the spark gone from the eyes of his old foe, but he was confident that the anti-unionist movement was dead. Such issues rest uneasily in the long memories of Nova Scotians, and the *Morning Chronicle* reflects this with the comment, "it was the policy of the people of Nova Scotia to make the best of the Union while it lasted."

Chapter 6 – Notes

1. Saunders, E.M., Editor; *The Life and Letters of the Right Hon. Sir Charles Tupper Bart.,K.C.M.G.* Vol. 1 London, Cassell and Company Ltd. 1916.

2. Sir Charles Hibbert Tupper, Sir Charles' second son, said that his father's life had also been threatened at this time.

3. Tupper had just received a note from McGee, penned just before his death, asking him to sell his novel, *Cyrus O'Neill*, to the London firm of Hurst and Blackett.

CHAPTER 7

Senior Physician and Politician

Tupper was a very busy man in 1867. He was a central figure in the move to Confederation. John A. Macdonald depended on him as the man who would win over many who were on the fence. But he was still the Premier of Nova Scotia and had many pressing local issues. He argued for better university education, better hospitals, and he continued his role as medical officer. His promotion since 1863 of a medical school in the Maritimes was at last bearing fruit in the closing days of 1867. In the same year he was involved in the discussions for a national medical society and was elected the founding president of the Canadian Medical Association.[1]

Canadian Medical Association

Despite his busy political schedule in the year of Confederation, Tupper continued his active role in medical issues. He travelled to Quebec for a meeting on 9 October 1867 at Laval University to discuss the organization of a national medical association.[2] Delegates had gathered from all over the new Dominion. Their first action was to elect a new president. Tupper was proposed and unanimously elected.

Tupper acknowledged the compliment and gave an "eloquent address" of acceptance. He said that he hoped their deliberations would show that "our leading objects are to protect the health and lives of the people of this Dominion from the unskilled treatment of incompetent men, and to provide in the most effective manner for the due qualification of the members of a profession as important as our own." With the new organization launched, he and the other members of the new society and their spouses set off to tour the Beauport Lunatic Asylum where they were met by Dr. Roy and Dr. Landry, and by the mayor and other dignitaries. The building was described as "a beautiful place, decorated with handiwork done by the patients and with flowers in many places." After a fine dinner, with many toasts, Tupper rose again and gave another speech. Feeling cheerful and proud of their participation in a new cooperative venture, the members climbed into thirty carriages and followed Tupper to the St. Louis Hotel for last libations and sleep.

Although this was an organizational meeting, the Canadian Medical Association was well and truly launched, but plans for the first annual meeting were yet to be made. It was decided to hold it in Montreal in September, 1868.[3, 4]

Tupper's first Presidential Address was an eloquent discourse on the profession of medicine, the importance of excellent medical education and a code of ethics.[5] His talk was interrupted on several occasions by applause and cheers. He thanked the society for the honour of serving them as President, and he looked forward to working with the new President. However, at the end of the meeting, when the nominating committee brought forward its slate of officers, Charles Tupper again headed the list for President.

In his *History of the Canadian Medical Association*,[6] H.E. MacDermot says that Dr. Marsden of Quebec had played the major role in organizing the meeting, but it was obvious that the Association had made a wise move in choosing Charles Tupper as its President. Tupper was later elected President for a third term, a decision the *Canadian Medical Journal* applauded. The journal said, "The conflicting interests of the profession in the various provinces sometimes sought expression in a manner hardly calculated to allay excitement, and medical politics at times ran high. Amid all the surrounding excitement the President was cool, and in matters of ruling never unprepared. His extensive Parliamentary experience gave his decisions weight and character, and the Association invariably submitted, showing the complete confidence they reposed in him."

After his three terms as President he was followed by Daniel MacNeill Parker, who had been his friend and fellow worker on issues such as the need for an office of statistics in Nova Scotia, and for his work in the Nova Scotia Medical Society. In his address of acceptance as President of the CMA, Parker acknowledged Tupper had admirably filled the chair and always acted impartially but with firmness, and had helped the Association through its growing pains. He mentioned that it was every physician's duty to contribute to society, especially since physicians had a background and capacity to add comment and advice in certain areas. But young physicians should be wary of a life in politics, even though there seemed to be a flood of doctors into legislatures, as it is difficult to serve two masters; political life might make a few medical statesmen, but many more spoiled doctors.[7]

Dalhousie Medical School

Tupper had long argued that there should be a medical school in the Maritimes. In 1863, when he was on the first Board of Dalhousie College, he impressed on the Board the important step recently taken in Kingston where a medical school at Queen's University had been founded. Whereupon Joseph Howe moved and Dr. Avery seconded the motion that discussions begin with the Medical Society about establishing a medical school. The physicians in the Medical Society, however, pointed out that there were insufficient hospital facilities for teaching and no legislation that would allow the dissection of human bodies. The matter did not arise again until late in 1867. At that time six local physicians reopened the proposal and made a submission to the Board of Dalhousie.[8, 9, 10]

When the Governors met on 14 January 1868, a letter was read from Dr. A. P. Reid of the Medical Society. The Board was not enthusiastic about the idea, and felt it might prove to be a great expense for the College. The Secretary was directed to answer Dr. Reid indicating that the Board had set up a committee to examine the proposal. Three days later the Board rejected the self-selected list of faculty, and Dr. Reid called another meeting of the physicians and surgeons to state that the list would have to be modified as two on the suggested list were not acceptable to the Board. No record exists of who was deemed unacceptable as faculty, and Reid's uncorroborated comment in the minutes was that this was not for any personal reasons. Private conversations were held by Reid with the two physicians and they agreed to resign "to favor success of the project." Although the way was now paved, the members of the faculty were not happy with the manner in which they had been treated by the Board, and although President Ross had previously expressed his desire for university faculties of law and medicine, the Board seemed cool to the proposal.

The Board committee reported back on the 12th of February, stating they "approved generally of the scheme." A second letter was read from a "proposed faculty," and another committee was struck to confer with the medical society and the letter's signatories.

On the 25th of February the Board approved a faculty of medicine with the cool statement that it "does not feel justified in refusing the offer of the gentlemen who proposed a form of Medical Faculty in connection with Dalhousie College, and the Faculty, being ready and desirous to receive students in the ensuing spring, the Board saw no sufficient reason for postponing further action on the matter." Dr. A. P. Reid was appointed President of the new faculty and Professor Lawson of Dalhousie as Dean. Tupper was pleased with the result but was not in attendance at these meetings as he had left for London to intercept Howe and his anti-confederation petition.

Dalhousie was now the fifth medical school in Canada. The time from the first meeting of the physicians, the organization of the curriculum and the teachers, the advertisement for students, to the beginning of the first class was less than five months, a record of administrative efficiency that would be unlikely today.

The Faculty was given one small room in the Dalhousie College building on the Grand Parade, with an anatomy room in the attic which lacked adequate light and could only be entered by a ladder through a trap door.[11] Announcements were made and a class of twelve students began on the 4th of May with lectures and anatomy dissection at the College, clinical lectures at the Provincial and City Hospital and at the City Dispensary, and autopsy experience at the Dead House.[12]

Initially the goal of the school was to reduce the great expense for maritime students travelling to Edinburgh, New York, Boston or Philadelphia for years of study, by providing the first two years of study in Halifax. The students would then travel to these centres to complete their MD. Two years later, however, the faculty felt they had the resources and teachers to provide a full course of medical studies for the MD degree and asked for the Board's approval in 1870. Dalhousie struck a committee to study the matter and appointed Dr. Tupper as chairman.[13] The committee recommended approval, legislation was secured, lecturers in the medical school were appointed to the rank of professor, and the first session of the full medical school began in November 1870. Of the 12 medical students attracted in 1868 for the initial years of study, five took the new opportunity to stay and complete their degree, while the other seven continued on to Harvard and New York.

Tupper and Parker were offered professorships in the new faculty by Dalhousie Board Chairman Justice William Young, on 3 July 1869. This is noted in Tupper's journal, but there is no indication that Tupper actually accepted or served.

Luggage and Louis Riel

An episode in the winter of 1869 involved Tupper as a man and as a father. Emma, the only daughter of Charles and Frances, married Captain D.R. Cameron of the Royal Artillery, in July 1869, and soon after their marriage Cameron was posted to Pembina in the Northwest Territories. He was assigned to accompany the Hon. William MacDougall who was to take over the government of the Territories when they were handed over to Canada on the 1st of December. In the meantime, Metis leader Louis Riel led a rebellion, seized Fort Garry, and set up a government there.

When MacDougall, accompanied by the newlyweds, arrived at the Hudson's Bay post north of Pembina, they were met by a band of 25 Metis with an order from Riel not to allow MacDougall to remain in the territory on pain of death. They returned to Pembina, a village of log and mud huts, while Capt. Cameron went on towards Fort Garry, leaving Emma and her maid at Scratching River. He was captured by a band of 300 Metis who took his horses, wagon and family baggage, and sent him back to Pembina.

Emma's anxiety increased with each event, and to make things worse for the bride she soon found herself alone again. Cameron had been called away by MacDougall, their manservant went off to

Fort Garry to see if he could retrieve their luggage, and the maid became so frightened she hurried back to Fort Garry as well. While Emma was alone, as Sir Charles tells it, "in stalked a strapping Indian, all war paint and feathers. She thought the best thing to do was to feed him. She cooked everything in the house - potatoes, meat and bread." When he was stuffed he indicated his satisfaction by patting his distended abdomen, laughed and left.

When her parents heard of these events they were alarmed at the danger for their only daughter, and Frances implored Charles to go and bring her home. Sir Charles immediately left by boat for New York, thence to Ottawa. On the way he met Donald A. Smith who had been appointed one of the Commissioners to deal with the Riel uprising. They arrived in Ottawa and met with Sir John A. Macdonald who said there were no more communications from Fort Garry, but he would value Tupper's observations on the uprising if he could get there.

On 13 December 1869, Tupper and Smith headed off by way of Toronto, Chicago, and St Cloud, Minnesota, to the end of the railway, then by stage to Fort Abercrombie and finally by dogsled to the isolated Hudson's Bay post at Georgetown. The temperature was -30 F (-35 C). They met up with a worried MacDougall who had not been out of his clothes in two months, hourly fearing for his life.

Tupper, thinking Smith and MacDougall might want to talk privately, went ahead towards the spot a mile distant where they were to camp for the night. Suddenly a band of Metis appeared in front of him. He had left his revolver in the sled and could not converse with them, as they spoke no English or French. He asked where they came from by gesture and they indicated Georgetown. They fingered his raccoon coat, talked among themselves and wandered off.

The party later moved by horse-drawn sled along the winding 600 miles from Fort Abercrombie to Pembina, south of Winnipeg, sleeping on buffalo hides in the deep snow and making fires from fallen branches. When they arrived at the log house where the Camerons were staying, Emma looked up at her father and asked, "What did you come for?"

The next day Tupper's medical skills were called upon when the postmaster's young daughter became ill. He diagnosed a hysterical attack which "yielded readily to treatment." Tupper wanted next to go to Fort Garry, as Sir John A. had requested, but Donald Smith protested that Tupper was identified with Confederation which was believed by Riel, and others in Fort Garry, to be the cause of all their troubles. Tupper persisted, so Smith said he would see what he could do to arrage the journey. Days later, hearing nothing, a frustrated and impatient Tupper decided to find someone who would take him. After a number of refusals he found a 17 year old lad who agreed to be his guide after Tupper offered to pay him anything he asked. He left secretly, taking only a buffalo skin, a bottle of sherry and a loaf of plain bread. Making their way past a nearby Hudson's Bay post, they stopped to borrow a toboggan, in case the snow got deep. To Tupper's surprise, Smith opened the door.

Tupper was irritated that Smith hadn't communicated with him, even though he was nearby. Smith said that Fort Garry was extremely dangerous now, as Riel had seized the fort and had all the guns and whisky. He told Tupper he was taking his life in his hands to go there since one man had been shot the day before. Smith knew this would not deter Tupper, who was known to be very impetuous and likely to do something rash. Smith again warned him not to go, but Tupper waved him off as he asked for the loan of a dog cariole for the journey.

On the way they encountered freezing fog. Tupper decided to continue although they couldn't see more than a few feet ahead, and had to follow the track by the feel under their feet. It was not long before they were lost. As the sky above was clear, Tupper could see the pole star and remembered being taught by his father when he was nine how to keep direction by the stars. Late that night they crossed the Red River and found a log cabin belonging to a Metis and his wife who welcomed them and fed them.

The next day they reached St. Norbert's Nunnery where they were met by two young nuns, Sister McGregor and Sister Riel, Louis Riel's sister. The Sister Superior said if he wished to send a message to Riel he could write a letter and they would get a messenger to deliver it. But when the messenger arrived Tupper got dressed and insisted the messenger take him in person.

At Fort Garry they were let in by password. There were a few hundred armed men with Riel in his Council Chamber, where he was talking with his advisors, Father Richot and Mr. Le May of Pembina.

On their arrival Riel approached Tupper and shook his hand, asking his business there. Tupper introduced himself as an independent member of the House of Commons, who came to ask for his daughter's seized horses, wagon and baggage. Riel said they would be restored to him the next day if he would wait at the house of the man who brought him. Tupper said he would be willing to go directly to the man who had his daughter's things, but Riel cut him off saying he could arrange this better than Tupper but would only do so if Tupper did as he was directed. Tupper agreed, thanked Riel and they shook hands.

That night he slept on the floor of the driver's house and next evening the trunks and effects, unopened, were delivered. At this point he met with Father Richot and indicated that he had another reason for coming beyond the "trifles" belonging to his daughter, which was to propose a resolution for the rebellion. Richot's English was no better than Tupper's French so they went to the nunnery for Sister MacDougall to interpret. The message was simple: the rebels could not succeed against Canada, but if they avoided bloodshed, they could get what they wanted by negotiation, and the leaders who accomplished this would be "entitled to great consideration".

Richot argued that the rebels would never be caught in the vast land they inhabited and besides, they could join the United States if things went against them. Tupper countered by stating flatly that the United States would not lift a hand to help the rebels as it would put them at war with England. Richot was impressed by the arguments, but said that one man must die, the one who had ordered a priest's assassination. Tupper said the man could be punished, but no blood was to be shed or the deal was off. [14]

They returned to Richot's house and Louis Riel and his advisor Mr. Le May came and spent the night. Riel discussed the situation with his advisors and agreed to receive a delegation from the Canadian Government, in the persons of Colonel de Salaberry and Father Thibeault. Tupper avoided anything but general conversation with them and left the next day. As he left the two Sisters came out and sang for him in Cree. [15]

Just as he was to leave another crisis arose. Mr. Le May got a message from his wife saying that he should bring Tupper immediately to Pembina, as his daughter had been attacked. On the journey

Tupper took the opportunity to convince Le May that negotiation with the Canadian Government was the only way to succeed. Later Le May wrote to Tupper saying that he was probably not aware that the populace was ready to lynch him in Pembina for arguing the case for negotiation.

As soon as he got back to Pembina, Tupper wrote to Sir John A. indicating he had paved the way for negotiations with Riel, but although Colonel de Salaberry and Father Thibeault would make some progress, he should send a statesman of stature and ability armed with large discretionary powers to close the deal. The ignominious treatment of Riel and his tragic end might have been different had Macdonald heeded Tupper's advice. To Tupper a deal was a deal, but Macdonald later reversed his stance.

Tupper took his daughter and son-in-law back to Ottawa and then continued on to Halifax, arriving on 28 January 1870 on the ship *City of Boston*.[16] Tupper noted that he had travelled thousands of miles by train, stage, horse, dog sled and on foot, slept in snow, tents and log cabin floors, taken his daughter out of danger, retrieved her belongings, met with Riel, laid the groundwork for a negotiated resolution of the rebellion - and returned home twenty pounds heavier!

Life in Ottawa

Tupper, with his family, settled down in Ottawa and resumed the practice of medicine. Soon after opening his Ottawa practice he had "obtained a place in the front rank of his profession" and "his income from this source, in spite of the distraction of political duties, amply sufficed for all his needs."[17]

By 1871, however, the Nova Scotia delegation in the House of Commons had grown considerably and was clamouring for Tupper's presence as their leader in cabinet. He was named President of the Council, then Minister of Inland Revenue, and later Minister of Customs. These portfolios were secondary to his personal power in cabinet, which was the product of his sharp mind, political acumen, total self-confidence, powers of persuasion and his closeness to John A. Macdonald. Macdonald repeatedly indicated his reliance on Tupper, not just for advice, but for his force on issues and his ability to persuade (some would say to pummel into submission) anyone who was standing in the way of government policy. Joseph Howe and John A. Macdonald were both brilliant politicians, but often with visions they felt unable to pursue for fear of backlash if they failed, or simply from their inability to overcome resistance. But Tupper, by contrast, was the enforcer, who could usually accurately size up a situation and judge if it was possible to overcome the opposition. Some said he was courageous, brilliant, undeterred in pursuing his principles and able to succeed where many would fail. Others saw him as a bully, a belligerent, humourless infighter who stopped at nothing to achieve his ends, especially if they involved his political agenda, his leader or his family. He was seen as Macdonald's biggest stick, and one who planned to set up a Tupper dynasty.

Vital Statistics

On St. Patrick's Day, 1876, Tupper rose in the House to complain that an item was missing from the budget estimates of the Department of Agriculture: $4,100 for the statistics office in Halifax. This was not merely a particularly perspicacious observation of a budget sheet, but part of a long-standing fight over a social process which Tupper felt was important for the health of the citizenry.

The General Registry was established in England in 1836 under the leadership of Dr. William Farr, often referred to as the father of statistics, who said, "Health was not only a state of physical well-being but also a reflection of the broader social and political circumstances in which men lived." Tupper strongly held this belief.

In Nova Scotia there had been various attempts to collect birth and death records since 1761. The clerks of townships without parishes were required to record births within 30 days or be fined five shillings. Otherwise church registries were depended on to keep accurate records. Despite these efforts, the recording of vital statistics was haphazard, and captured only 20% of the deaths. A memorandum from Lord Grey outlining the recommendations of the Registrar General for an effective census stimulated the introduction of a bill in the Nova Scotia Legislature in 1849, which passed after much wrangling in 1850. A Board of Statistics was set up but appeared to stop functioning after an unsuccessful attempt at a census in 1851. An effort to revive the process failed in 1858, and there was little interest in the suggestion Tupper received from Patrick Monaghan offering to establish a private, non-governmental system if a subsidy were provided. Bills failed again in 1860 and 1861, partly due to high cost estimates, and partly because of opposition from some groups such as the Central Baptist Association. In 1861 a bill to establish a Halifax-based central registration system failed, but a census of the province was carried out that year, showing a population of 330,857. Causes of death during the census period were listed, linking health to census as emphasized by Farr, to provide an informative picture of the health of the populace.

Frustrated by the lack of a permanent registration system, Charles Tupper spoke at the October meeting of the Medical Society of Nova Scotia, suggesting they take on the recording of causes of death since the legislature couldn't make its mind up. The Society agreed, but on petitioning the legislature it received only lukewarm reception, and for the next six years annual attempts at passage of a bill on this issue failed. Undeterred, Tupper, Daniel MacNeil Parker, W. J. Lewis and other physicians, supported by the Medical Society, continued to argue for a permanent registration and statistical system; a bill was entered again in 1864, and during this debate Tupper unsuccessfully argued for some remuneration for the doctors who would be required to determine cause of death. Although the bill was amended in debate Tupper was satisfied enough with the result, if only to get a system in place. In attacking Adams George Archibald, who objected to the centralization of the process, Tupper lashed out in his aggressive style and eventually the bill passed. Dr. Lewis was appointed Secretary of the Board of Statistics at a salary of $800 per annum, and was later succeeded by John Costley. From that time to Confederation three years later Nova Scotia collected vital statistics. Although the system was improving, it was not without its deficiencies.

The British North America Act (1867) gave responsibility for statistics and census to the federal government. Surprisingly, the responsibility was placed under the Department of Agriculture. The Nova Scotia Board of Statistics continued but with support from the federal department. Unfortunately, jealousies and jurisdictional arguments arose between the provincial and federal offices which impaired the work of each registry. The report of 1870 showed great improvement in the recording information and, among other useful data, it showed the province to have 262 doctors, 69 druggists, 20 dentists, 200 lawyers, and 897 churches, serving a population of 387,300.

In the next few years arguments over who was responsible for paying deputy registrars arose which led to an attempt by the federal government to close down the Halifax office. The Halifax Registrar, John Costley, would lose his job, despite his excellent leadership, to be replaced, as Tupper snarled, "with a clerk in the office far inferior to him physically and intellectually." Tupper was overly harsh as the replacement, the Rev. Hugh MacMillan, set a very high standard in the next few years. [18]

By 1881 support for a strengthened federal system of statistics was evident in Nova Scotia and supported by the Canadian Medical Association. Dr. Daniel MacNeil Parker continued to argue for a registry office in Halifax, and over the next twenty years the Maritime Medical News sporadically supported him. Not until 1908 was a bill introduced by Premier Murray that would re-establish, after a 31 year gap, a Registry of Vital Statistics. Tupper lived to see the long fight that he and his colleagues had led finally succeed.

President of Council

The first few years of government after confederation were stormy, and in 1870 Sir John A. insisted that Tupper should join his government. In a speech to the House in 1870 Tupper made mention of his concept of a National Policy, a concept that was to guide the government for the next decades. After this speech Macdonald urged Tupper to join the cabinet, which he did as President of the Council once he was assured that a majority of the Nova Scotia members would support him.

The first issues to interest Tupper in his new role were the Intercontinental Railway, the arguments about fisheries fees for US boats in Canadian waters and the attempts to renew the lapsed Reciprocity Treaty with the United States. In an argument over whether the bridges on the railway should be constructed of wood or iron, Tupper agreed with Sir Sandford Fleming that iron was the best long-term solution, and reversed the decision of the Chairman of Commissioners who had put out tenders for wooden bridges. On the fisheries issue (an old fight for him), he sent a telegram to Macdonald to say that selling major fishing rights to the USA especially for short-term gain, would be regarded by Canadians as equivalent to giving up territory. Agreements must protect Canadian rights, Tupper argued, and any arrangements should be in exchange for substantial funds. A treaty was signed in 1872 protecting Canada's fishing rights.

In the general election of 1872 Tupper and Howe swept Nova Scotia, and each was elected by acclamation. Tupper could by then survey the political scene and recognize that his efforts were successful. Anti-confederation was a dead issue.

Howe was by now an ageing figure in Ottawa. He no longer had the spark or held the power that had made him so formidable in Nova Scotia politics. When it was clear that his health was failing Tupper discussed with the Prime Minister the possibility of Howe's appointment as Lieutenant-Governor of Nova Scotia. Macdonald agreed, and on his recommendation the appointment was ratified by the Queen. Howe had long cherished the idea of this position and was grateful to Tupper for his kindness. Before leaving Ottawa Howe said at a farewell champagne luncheon, "Boys, I want you to stand by Tupper, as he has stood by me." He took up his duties in Government House in Halifax but three weeks later he was dead.

Life as a Cabinet Minister

Tupper resigned as President of Council and was appointed Minister of Inland Revenue. He had been recommended for knighthood but he informed Sir John A. Macdonald that he had no wish to receive the K.C.M.G. (Knight Commander of the Order of St. Michael and St. George) if Howe was not also knighted. Howe did not live to receive this honor, but Tupper would later be recognized.

While in Ottawa Tupper again had established a medical practice, as was his habit wherever he was living, and the income from medicine was equal to or greater than that of cabinet minister.

In 1871 he leased "Armdale," his home in Halifax near the Northwest Arm, an area that now has taken to itself the name of Armdale.[19] In the fall of 1871 he moved with Frances and his granddaughter Sophie Cameron who was very ill, to their new summer place, "Highland Hill," in Saint Andrew's, New Brunswick.[20] Saint Andrew's was more convenient from Montreal and Ottawa, as it was on the rail line, whereas Halifax had yet to be connected to Quebec by rail.

The Pacific Scandals

Although he was busy as a federal cabinet minister, Tupper's interest in political events in his home province never waned, but his interest was not always welcomed as he was not reluctant to interfere. There was opposition by the repeal government of Nova Scotia to the power of such federal politicians as Tupper, who, it was feared, could influence local provincial elections. The provincial government therefore enacted a law to curb their involvement during election campaigns. When Tupper became embroiled in an effort to resist the legislation, a motion of censure was entered against him in the House of Commons by Alexander MacKenzie. Tupper dismissed the criticism by responding that certain members were simply supporting the anti-unionists in Nova Scotia; the motion was defeated. A greater scandal was brewing, however; although Tupper was not involved, it would take down the government.

Sir Hugh Allan was attempting to head the company that would build the Canadian Pacific Railroad to the west. The politicians in Ottawa with whom he negotiated did not know that Allan was connected with Jay Gould in the USA. Gould wanted to claim the west for the United States. While Allan was negotiating with London for funding, he was secretly arranging deals with the Americans. Allan would be given the position as president of the railway, but the politicians, with George Etienne Cartier as spokesman, wanted some political funding for so rich an arrangement. As revealed later, in letters sold by one of the American backers to the highest bidder (in this case the Liberals), Cartier asked for kickbacks for six leading members of the Conservative Party. [21]

Parliament was becoming disruptive and Macdonald was losing his political control during the debates, unable to answer the public outcry about the "Pacific Scandals." Lord Dufferin, the Governor General, planned to ask Macdonald to resign, but Tupper, now Minister of Customs, met with him and said it would be the mistake of his life, as his responsibility was to represent the Queen and not take political sides. When the Governor General asked what he should do, Tupper suggested he frankly give his opinion of matters to the Colonial Office, but withdraw his request for Macdonald's resignation; this he did. Things had gone beyond the point of salvage, however, and soon Macdonald tendered his resignation. Tupper could at least be satisfied that it came about by the proper process. This was not the last time Tupper would see a Governor General overstepping the bounds of political rectitude.

The CPR scandal was hardly defensible and Macdonald had resigned in favour of the Liberals; in the 1874 election called by the new Prime Minister, Alexander MacKenzie, Macdonald and the Conservatives were routed. MacKenzie's term in office was characterized by inactivity, economic depression and political paralysis. Little was done on the railroad, which was slowly being built in a piecemeal fashion as each region could afford it.

After the fall of the Macdonald government in 1873, Tupper the physician and Macdonald the lawyer resumed their professions, while sitting on the opposition side of the House.[22] Tupper rented a house on Metcalfe Street in Ottawa, formerly occupied by the Hon. Peter Mitchell, and subsequently by Sir Albert Smith. There, "quietly and unostentatiously," said the Ottawa Citizen, he "hung out his shingle in the customary way." He moved briefly to Toronto because he and Frances were concerned about the health of their son William who was distraught over the death of his wife in childbirth. He established a thriving consulting practice on the corner of Jarvis and Queen Streets in Toronto. Once satisfied that William was getting over his wife's death, he responded to a call from Ottawa and plunged into the political fray again. When Sir Charles informed Frances they would be moving from Toronto back to Ottawa she replied that, because they were being treated so kindly, it was "more than it is worth to leave Toronto." In spite of her reluctance, they returned to Ottawa where he again set up a medical practice, with prominent patients such as Lord Dufferin, the Governor General.

The next few years were lacklustre for Tupper in his role in opposition as finance critic, but he played the part of a senior leader in the House. He spoke against the government's piecemeal approach to the building of the railway, and gave what many have believed was one of the greatest speeches of his career. It lasted 4 hours, and in it he criticized the wasteful spending and the lack of vision of the Liberal government for a railroad that was the thread to tie the country together. In a subsequent speech by Tupper in Kingston, Macdonald was to follow as the main drawing card, but when he rose to speak he endorsed everything that had been said by

Tupper in his "peculiar manner – a manner in which no man can approach him in the whole Dominion of Canada." He went on to say that his place as leader could well be filled by Tupper. When he later offered to step down in Tupper's favour, after his party went down to defeat, Tupper said if Macdonald resigned he would as well.

Tupper had coined the term "National Policy" to encompass the concepts that he felt would bind and protect the nation. On 22 February 1877 Macdonald moved and Tupper seconded a motion for the adoption of a National Policy which would provide tariffs to protect small industry, mining, agriculture and other businesses that otherwise could not prosper in competition with the United States. With an election brewing, Tupper began an energetic schedule of speeches throughout Ontario and the Maritimes, outlining the importance of the National Policy. The National Policy appealed to many voters before the 1878 election. At the time there was a depression many believed would be corrected by the protection of small businesses and by the completion of a railroad that would open up opportunities and markets in the west and convince British Columbia to stay in the confederation.

The next year, 1878, the Conservatives were returned to power with a sizeable majority.[23] Macdonald was now tired and turned even more to the strength of Tupper. Tupper was appointed Minister of Railroads and Canals, and was now able to play out his vision of the railroad as a major instrument in the building of the nation.[24]

A Railway *A Mare Usque Ad Mare*

Tupper now had the opportunity and the responsibility of rejuvenating the CPR project. It had to be soundly funded and put back on schedule with firm deadlines. In 1879, with Macdonald and Tilley, he sailed for London to seek financial backing, but was unsuccessful as the British thought it was a risky scheme that might go bankrupt, just as the nervous MacKenzie government had suspected. It was Tupper's feeling that the only way to get the project rolling was to bring in a syndicate of major financiers. He requested and received the consent of the Privy Council to negotiate with "capitalists of undoubted means," a Canadian-American syndicate, and to barter tax concessions and tracts of land to sweeten the speculative deal with investors. The concessions were huge, estimated at 260 million dollars, but the project was up and running and came in under the deadline.

Such wheeling and dealing, especially necessary when the government was anxious for sound financial backing, invited opposition and public suspicion of the rapid, quiet negotiations. Despite their different personalities, Macdonald and Tupper had worked well together ever since their first collaboration in Charlottetown fifteen years earlier. At this juncture, with important national policies to pursue, the two old colleagues needed each other's support more than ever. Sadly, it was at this point they had a major falling out.

There are differences of opinion on the event that precipitated their disagreement, and there may have been more than one. It is clear in the correspondence between Charles Hibbert Tupper and Joseph Pope that the two men did not see eye-to-eye over the plans for the railroad. The government was embarrassed at having to provide more money for the railroad after being promised that no more would be needed, and Macdonald asked Tupper for his proposals on how the government was to deal with all of this. Tupper outlined his views but his response also included an extension of the eastern end of the railway to Sydney, in Cape Breton. This was an important part of Tupper's concept which included his promise, especially to Nova Scotians, of a railroad sea to sea. Sir John A. angrily said it wasn't possible. Tupper said he was Minister of Railroads and wouldn't submit his proposals without it. Macdonald protested he would not have a pistol pressed to his breast. Tupper snapped that he had stood between the pistol and Sir John A.'s breast most of his political life, and stomped out of the Council chambers and returned to his office to pack his things. Bowell and Pope went after him and convinced him not to leave. As had happened so often before in any debate, Tupper eventually won. Sir John A. gave in and apologized but they each bore a long lasting resentment. The rift between the two men persisted. Charles Hibbert Tupper, his son, said that when they sat together there was nothing but the business of government between them.[25]

Even though the dates don't fit, others have suggested the rift was really about passing government work to his son. It was said that Tupper insisted the government send some business by way of his son's Winnipeg law firm – which also happened to be Macdonald's son's firm.

Whatever the cause – and the railroad episode was certainly the likely event – there was a cooling of the relationship between the two friends. For most of their careers Macdonald had depended on Tupper. In the next two years Tupper would need the support of Macdonald, but they were not on easy speaking terms.

One deal that became public landed Tupper in hot water. A tender for a stretch of railroad in British Columbia went to Andrew Onderdonk, even though his bid was $209,255 higher than the lowest. Tupper answered the opposition criticism and charges of government underhandedness by saying the $20,000 deposit cheque from the lower bid was irregular, and thus unacceptable. It had been marked "good for two days only." But it became known that Tupper also had a bank letter assuring him that the phrase could be struck out as the cheque would be honoured at any time. Although no evidence of wrongdoing was ever produced, and the Onderdonk contract was passed by a vote of 125 to 55, a shadow fell over Tupper, and the government had no desire to remind the public of the CPR scandals of the past. Meanwhile a secret arrangement was made to allow Tupper to be appointed High Commissioner to London. It may have been intended as a gentle, dignified means of putting the old warhorse out to pasture, but the appointment turned out to be an even greater embarrassment to the government.

Although still a member of parliament and a cabinet minister, he now had a second job, a situation forbidden by the Independence of Parliament Act. The government weakly defended its position by admitting that he indeed held two positions, as cabinet minister and high commissioner, but this was allowable as he only received pay for one, the cabinet post. This did not impress the opposition, so a writ of $5000 for infringement of the Act was served on Tupper. To save his hide the government passed an amendment that allowed Tupper to hold both positions as long as he was paid for only one of them.

In the spring of 1884 Tupper left to take up his duties in London, no doubt believing he was leaving party politics behind.

Chapter 7 – Notes

1. At the entrance of the Canadian Medical Association Building at 1867 Alta Vista Drive (an appropriate street number) there is a bust of Sir Charles Tupper and an identical bust in the foyer of the Sir Charles Tupper Medical Building at Dalhousie University. In 1995 the living presidents of the Canadian Medical Association unveiled a granite stone at his grave site in Halifax with a plaque, indicating his contributions as founding President of the CMA, to match the plaque placed nearby by the Government of Canada.

2. One hundred and sixty-four physicians gathered at Laval University, Quebec city, 100 days after Confederation, on 9 October 1867. (Waugh, Douglas; *Much Done, Much To Do: The CMA Turns 125*, Canad. Med Assoc J, 1992; 147:1064-1067.)

3. Tupper served three terms as President of the Canadian Medical Association, initially called the Canadian Medical Society. He is the only president in its history to have served more than one term.

4. Tupper's membership card for that meeting is in the Tupper papers in the Provincial Archives of Nova Scotia (PANS), and has Tupper's signature as President, with two representatives, a vice-president and a secretary from each of the four colonies in the confederation. At the meeting Nova Scotia was also represented by two colleagues; one was James R. DeWolfe from Tupper's Edinburgh days and a prominent Halifax physician, and the other was Dr. Rufus S. Black. After three terms as president he would be followed by his friend, Dr. Daniel MacNeil Parker.

5. This address is included in its entirety as Appendix 2.

6. MacDermot, H.E., *History of the Canadian Medical Association 1867-1921*, Toronto, Murray Printing Company Limited, 1935.

7. Parker, William Frederick, *Daniel MacNeill Parker: His Ancestry and a Memoir of His Life*, Toronto, William Briggs. 1910. Page 222.

8. Murray, T.J. and Murray, Suellen; *The History of Dalhousie Medical School*, MeDal, Part 1, 12-14, 1982-1983 issue. Part 2, 7-9, 1983-1984 issue. Part 3, 8-10, 1984-1985 issue. Part 4, 5-11, 1985-1986 issue.

9. In the minutes of this meeting they referred to themselves as the Faculty of Medicine. For that reason some have erroneously noted 1867 as the founding date of the medical school rather than 1868 when the faculty was accepted by the Board of Governors of Dalhousie.

10. The six who met on 10 December 1867 were Doctors Hattie, Slayter, Sommers, Reid, Farrell and Woodhill.

11. The anatomy room had a slanted roof that did not allow students to stand erect, was poorly ventilated and dark. The smell was terrible and the students continually rubbed their hands with lavender oil. John Wilson, a letter carrier, was entrusted with the procurement of bodies, but this was often done by ruse and with the assistance of the students. They had an arrangement with the Poor Asylum for the acquisition of the bodies of those who died without kin. Daniel MacIntosh, one of the first graduating class of 1872, described 50 years later the switching of the body in the coffin with cordwood and carrying the corpse in a bag to a wagon, which sped off for the medical school. He described how three students tried to get the body up the ladder and through the trapdoor, when they all fell to the floor. "Then followed an indiscriminate flight for safety. After recovering our equanimity we carried the body to the dissecting room and the next day we were at work."

12. Students paid fees for each class and obtained tickets that confirmed payment. The fee for each class was $6.00. A demonstrator's fee was $4.00. The matriculation fee was $1.00. Two tickets for any class would entitle the holder to a perpetual ticket for that class with the exception of a demonstrator's fee.

13. Although never on the faculty of the medical school as he was then the Premier of the province, Tupper was instrumental at all stages of the formation of the school. He was on the active staff of the City and Provincial Hospital where clinical teaching would occur, and he was the leading advocate for improvements in hospital care at that institution. For these reasons the new Dalhousie medical school building of 1967 was named the Sir Charles Tupper Medical Building, the Centennial project of Nova Scotia. It recognized his dual role in Confederation and in the formation of the medical school.

14. A point by point discussion between Richot and Tupper is outlined in E.M. Saunder's *Life and Letters of the Right Hon. Sir Charles Tupper, Bart. K.C.M.G.*, with an introduction by the Right Hon. Sir R. L. Borden, K.C.M.G. London, Cassel and Company, Ltd. 1916.

15. Tupper corresponded with Sister Riel until her death many years later, and he visited Sister MacDougall each time he was in Winnipeg.

16. The ship then sailed for Liverpool but disappeared, never to be heard from again.

17. Longley, p. 104.

18. Dunlop, Allan; *Vital Statistics in Nova Scotia*. Unpublished manuscript PANS.

19. Tupper's home still stands, much enlarged, with extensions added over the years to make it a group of apartments.

20. The summer home, Highland Hill, is now an Inn called Tara, on the road into St. Andrew's. It has been expanded with multiple holiday cottages. Earlier in this century it was owned by the Hon. C. D. Howe.

21. Sir George E. Cartier ($50,000 and $25,000); Sir John A. Macdonald ($25,000 and $10,000); the Hon. Hector Langevin ($15,000). The American backer, George McMullin, received $20,000 from the Conservatives to keep the issue quiet, but got a better offer of $37,500 from the Liberals.

22. Ad Multos Annon, by HJM. The Citizen, Ottawa, May 25, 1900. Public Archives of Nova Scotia, file 6225, Scrapbook Vol. XV, p. 195.

23. Tupper's win appears to have been a popular one. In *The Story of Dartmouth*, by John P. Martin, (privately printed, Dartmouth, NS, 1957) we are told of Tupper's triumphant welcome in Halifax. He was met by a giant torchlight procession and when, later that night, he took the ferry across Halifax Harbour to Dartmouth, he was met by another torchlight procession led by 150 men on horseback. There were bonfires along the way, houses were brilliantly lit in welcome, people joined the parade in carriages, and a large crowd accompanied them on foot. There were congratulations and speeches of welcome to Dr. Tupper, who responded in kind, and then the whole procession paraded through the streets to "Beechwood", the beautiful home of Tupper's friend Dr. Daniel Parker MacNeill.

24. On their arrival back in Ottawa, the Tuppers were presented with a portrait of Sir Charles painted for the citizens of Ottawa by R. I. Colin Forbes, R.C.A.

25. Letter from Joseph Pope to Charles Hibbert Tupper, Public Archives of Nova Scotia p. 3404.

CHAPTER 8

A Trace of Albumin

"Then there is Charles Tupper . . . broad shouldered,
self-contained, vigorous looking as Wellington's charger
'Copenhagen'. . . in repose, even, he looks as if he had a
blizzard secreted somewhere about his person."

George Ross [1]
Liberal

During the period 1878 to 1884, when the Conservatives had returned to power and Tupper was busy selling the National Policy, scrambling to fund the CPR and get the railroad built on time, he felt vigorous and appeared energetic and strong, especially to those who were on the other side of a question or in his way. George Ross, a Liberal member from 1873 to 1883, said he was "the most fearless combatant that ever sat in the Parliament of Canada. He was the 'Coeur de Lion' of the house," and he noted that when he had suffered one of Tupper's attacks he "left me wondering if I really had any definite opinions on public questions or was even remotely qualified to be a party politician." Tupper's vigour and force were legendary and feared. But by now, the apparent strength, the stentorian voice and the unlimited energy were beginning to show signs of wear and tear, if not to his parliamentary colleagues, at least to his physicians.

Tupper and Osler

In The New York Medical Journal, 23 November 1901, under the title "On the Advantages of a Trace of Albumin and a Few Tube Casts in The Urine of Certain Men Above Fifty Years of Age," Sir William Osler wrote:

Year by year I see an increasing number of cases which justify the somewhat paradoxical heading of this brief paper. He then described the unhealthy effects of rushed and busy schedules on business and professional men, such as the appearance of albumin and casts in the urine. These are not necessarily ominous, he said, although many physicians think they signal Bright's disease. They may only be nature's danger signal to slow down, like the red lights on the railroad. The person who lives fast and hard, with good food, liquor and cigars, ignoring the effect on the body, will deteriorate like the No. 15 yard engine being driven like the No 580, the mighty express train.

Osler developed the train analogy at great length, concluding that "careless stoking with high pressure for 25 years and bad treatment of his machine mean early degenerations, and his waste-pipes – kidneys – are often the first to show signs of ill usage" – a slight trace of albumin and a few tube casts in the urine.

Osler then described the case of "a very distinguished man in public life in Canada" who was found to have albumin and tube casts in his urine when applying for additional life insurance. The man was nearly 60 and leading a very active life, but he had been careless in his habits of eating and drinking. This prominent politician was very anxious and distressed when told that his career would be cut short because of this finding by his physician, Dr. R.P. Howard. [2] Dr. Howard referred the man to his former student, William Osler. Years later, in his obituary of Sir Charles Tupper, Osler revealed that the subject of the paper was Tupper. Osler then made the unusual comment that "in the summer of 1881 I went to England on the same steamer with him, and in London I discussed his condition with Sir Andrew Clarke, who took a very sombre view of the case." Despite the poor prognoses of his teacher and the noted English consultant, Osler believed the condition was benign and noted in his paper twenty years later that after a year of rest the politician got over his fright, resumed work, and accomplished as much in the following twenty years as he had in the previous twenty years. He commented, "He is still alive – an octogenarian of exceptional vigour."

Osler believed he had made an important observation, separating a benign warning of a rushed life from fatal Bright's disease, and said in his paper on Tupper, "I do not wish to minimize the importance of the information to be obtained by an examination of the urine, but we must ever bear in mind the adage – true to-day as well as in the times of the old "Pisse-Prophets"; *urina est meretrix, vel mendax* – the urine is a harlot or a liar."

Fourteen years after the publication and 34 years after the original consultation, Sir William Osler revealed the identity of his distinguished patient.

Sir Charles was 58 when he consulted Osler, a young but rising physician aged 31. Tupper was by then a national figure, a Father of Confederation, second in prominence and power in the new Dominion to the Prime Minister, Sir John A. Macdonald. Despite their difference in age, they were able to combine a respectful friendship with a medical relationship for the next 34 years. It has been said that Osler didn't like Tupper because Osler believed that Tupper tried to serve two masters, the medical profession and politics, and Osler felt this was inappropriate.[3] Osler clearly meant the opposite, and said so in his obituary of Tupper, confirmed by Osler's biographer, Harvey Cushing.[4]

In fact, Osler felt it was important for physicians to involve themselves in politics, in order to change things in a larger society.[5] Virchow, born the same year as Tupper, all his career was an influential pathologist and a local politician; he said that politics was but medicine on a grand scale. The views of Virchow were well known to Osler, who visited Virchow after he had completed his medical degree and was spending time travelling and studying in Europe. What Osler actually said was, "His (Tupper's) life is an illustration of the brilliant success of the doctor in politics. We have to go to France or to the South American Republic to parallel his career. He never really served two masters; from 1855 he was a politician first, and a practitioner only when stranded by the exigencies of party."

Osler makes clear his attitude towards physician patients and physicians in politics, and specifically to Tupper:

A doctor who comes to me with broken nerves is always asked two questions – it is unnecessary to ask about drink, as to the practised eye that diagnosis is easy – about Wall Street, and politics. It is astonishing how many doctors have an itch to serve the state in parliament, but for a majority of them it is a poor business which brings no peace to their souls. There is only one way for a doctor in political life – to belong to the remnant, the saving remnant of which Isaiah speaks, that votes for men not for parties, and that sees equal virtues (and evils) in 'Grits' and Conservatives. I have had one political principle (and practice), I always change with the Government. It keeps the mind plastic and free from prejudice. You cannot serve two masters, and political doctors are rarely successful in either career. There are great exceptions, for example Sir Charles Tupper a first-class surgeon in his day and a politician of exceptional merit. Nor do I forget that the great Clemenceau is a graduate in medicine of Paris, and that we have three members of the profession in the Imperial Cabinet, one of them a professor of anatomy at McGill. All the same, let the average man who has a family to support and a practice to keep up, shun politics as he would drink and speculation. As a right-living, clear-thinking citizen with all the interests of the community at heart the doctor exercises the best possible sort of social and political influence.[5]

Osler travelled to London with Tupper, who was wondering if his career was at an end.[6] Osler arranged a consultation with Sir Andrew Clarke, "who took a very sombre view of the case." Indeed, Sir Andrew took a sombre view of any busy politician, and of the lifestyle of those who live fast in defiance of the Laws of Health. Clarke had written on renal disease, including a paper on renal disease characterized by albumin and casts but with no pathological change in the kidney, which would respond to a restricted diet – a condition others would later say was non-existent.[7]

Sir Andrew assumed a prominent, busy politician would have health disorders related to excesses of diet, alcohol and work.[8] His dietary views and his dietary advice, (hardly "restrictions" as he called them), amounted to huge amounts of food daily. Like Osler, he did not think it inappropriate for a physician of such undoubted talents as Tupper to be a politician, but he believed that caution in life style was necessary, including avoidance of "hurry, worry, scurry, strain and lifting." In business or politics, one should have a "quiet, regular, occupied, tranquil life," and retire to bed early. None of this was characteristic of Sir Andrew himself, who had a backbreaking schedule. In fact, when at last Clarke had a fatal stroke many of his colleagues felt it was in part a result of his hectic schedule. Although he himself avoided daily politics, he did believe in speaking out on political issues that were socially relevant, particularly if they related to education, temperance, religion and morals, or social and sanitary reform, or hospital support and the like, and he was often an enthusiastic speaker at medical meetings.

At this time Tupper was recovering from an attack of bronchitis, and a band-like tightness around the head, "which rendered him unequal to any work." Although today tension-type headache would seem a likely diagnosis, Sir Andrew suggested "suppressed gout." He recommended a healthy regimen and gave him a prescription for a syrup of hypophosphate (Fellow's Solution). Tupper was puzzled by the suggestion that his ill health was due to his lifestyle, particularly strong drink... "I could hardly believe it," he said in his journal, "as I had been a very abstemious man, and my father had been still more so." Both Osler and Clarke assumed that Tupper was worn down by overeating, excess alcohol and a rushed life, but their assumption was probably based on the pattern they felt characterized a man in public and professional life, as it was rumoured to be the case for Macdonald, McGee and Howe. Tupper had a heavy schedule but he was always physically strong and vigorous, set aside a great deal of time for his family, ate moderately and used alcohol rarely.

Tupper had some trouble having Clarke's prescription filled, but he steadily improved on the strict health regimen. He was also probably depressed; his colleague George E. Cartier had died of Bright's disease and his father, the Reverend Charles, had recently died. But with the promise of renewed health on Sir Andrew's regime and William Osler's reassurance that his was a benign disease that would respond to a more controlled life, Sir Charles reassumed a busy public life. [9]

High Commissioner

In 1883 Sir Alexander Galt wished to retire as High Commissioner to London. Although the position was offered to Tupper, Macdonald was not happy to see him step down as Minister of Railways and Canals and as a Cabinet Minister, so he asked Tupper to accept the new position without salary.

The Tuppers took up the responsibilities as Canadian High Commissioner in June 1884 and established themselves at 97 Cromwell Road. He acknowledged that his role was to "watch, defend and guide the interests of the Dominion." Free of the banter and bruising of politics, Tupper expected to enjoy life in England. Although he had become accustomed to the relative egalitarianism of life in Canada, he had an admiration of things British. He had developed many friendships in England over the years and he fitted in well on the fringe of Parliament and in the life around Court. He had an income of $10,000, which was $2,000 more than the Prime Minister.

One of his first altercations in England in his new role was just the kind of fight he liked, bringing to the fore his tough approach, his medical training and his delight in showing the backbone of the colonies.

Three shiploads of cattle from Canada were stopped in Liverpool by inspectors who said they were infected with splenic fever and, perhaps, Texas fever. The whole cargo was to be slaughtered, and therefore Canadian cattle prevented from entering the country. From his knowledge of Mr. Moore, the inspector, and suspecting this was a form of protectionism against Canadian trade, Sir Charles quickly obtained letters from the Secretary of the Privy Council to Professor Duguid, the veterinary surgeon in charge, to give him access to all evidence and the facilities to examine the animals. Under his direction, Sir Charles had six animals slaughtered in his presence and personally demonstrated that they were free of any disease. Animals from the other ships were examined in a similar manner. Sir Charles demanded that Professor Duguid send an amended report immediately to London, allowing the ships to release their cargo without restriction. Sir John A. Macdonald wrote:

> I congratulate you most heartily on your skilful and successful action in saving our live cattle trade. The Press has already got

hold of it here, and I shall take an early opportunity of speaking of it publicly. No use hiding one's light under a bushel, eh?

After a year he visited Ottawa to report on his activities. While in Canada he travelled to Nova Scotia via Moncton. There he was entertained by the members of the CPR syndicate. In gratitude for his efforts in fostering the concept of a totally Canadian route across the continent, he was given a gift of stock in the CPR valued at $100,000 which he was able to accept as he was no longer a member of the government and therefore was not restricted from receiving gifts.

There was concern in the cabinet over who could replace the powerful Tupper. Some felt that John Thompson might be such a man, but he had been recently appointed to the Supreme Court in Nova Scotia. Although young for the bench, his cause was successfully championed in Ottawa by the very political Bishop Cameron of Antigonish. Thompson had represented Antigonish in the Nova Scotia Legislature and was an anti-confederate until he was brought over to the government side by Howe after he switched to the Conservatives. Macdonald and many others tried in vain to convince Thompson to consider a Cabinet post in government. Macdonald asked Tupper, on his arrival from London, to use his powers of persuasion on Thompson. Tupper recognized that the key to convincing Thompson, would be having him feel this was agreeable to Mrs. Thompson and to Bishop Cameron.

Thompson told those who pressured him that he would not accept such an offer unless the Bishop concurred. Thompson was a convert to Catholicism, and was beholden to the Bishop for his judgeship. The powerful and politically astute Bishop Cameron had such a hold on Thompson that when he was elected to the Legislature, J.W. Longley dubbed him "the Member for Bishop Cameron." Tupper first spoke to Mrs. Thompson and obtained her concurrence. He then met with Bishop Cameron. It is likely the two strong personalities, Cameron and Tupper, understood each other in such negotiations, and Tupper was able to get the Bishop's agreement for Thompson to resign the judgeship and enter the Cabinet. Tupper didn't stop there, however, but advised Thompson not to accept anything less than the position of Minister of Justice. This put Macdonald on the spot as that portfolio was filled by Campbell who wasn't ready to resign. However, it was arranged, and Thompson entered Government.

Charles and Frances Tupper, accompanied by Daniel Parker, Andrew Robertson and others left on a busy tour to many of the communities across the country, reaching the end of the railroad in British Columbia. Parker describes Tupper as being in fine form, polishing off any critics in public speeches, and being greeted with three cheers in each town. "Tupper was never better....He eats, drinks and sleeps well and is enjoying the journey immensely. Of course he is king out here. People think they owe their Canadian Pacific Railway to him, and this has given him a strong hold on the popular voice, as also among the better class."

On his return to London, Tupper heard he had been awarded the Knight Commander of the Order of St. Michael and St. George (K.C.M.G.), which did not excite all of his old colleagues at home, some of whom felt he was being rewarded over them. And rewarded he was, as he was also given an honorary degree by Cambridge University and on the same day an ancient honor from one of the City of London guilds, the Freedom of the Fishmongers' Company.

In his correspondence with Sir John A. he was pleased to hear that John Thompson was doing well in Ottawa, but unhappy that W. S. Fielding had won handsomely in Nova Scotia, a triumph for the anti-confederation movement that was again raising its head. In addition, problems were developing on the CPR and Tupper offered to return if that would help. Sir John A. was very worried about the party's standing heading for a general election in 1887, and with the consent of all his colleagues requested that Tupper resign as High Commissioner and return home to the Cabinet as Minister of Finance. Tupper ran for election in Cumberland and he and his party won easily. Soon afterwards he was back in England, negotiating the financing of the CPR again, but had to return to fight a court challenge to his election. A witness said that a Tupper supporter had paid a 50 cent railroad ticket for a man from Springhill. No personal charges were laid, but the election was declared void. The election was held again and Tupper did even better, increasing his margin from 611 to 1260.

The Tuppers crossed the Atlantic a number of times during these years, as he was often called upon by Sir John A. to help with crises at home and in England – and he always responded. In England he was again involved in discussions about the fisheries, an unresolved tension between the United States and the colonies of Britain that had gone on for over a century; in Canada Macdonald discussed with him the possibility of Newfoundland joining the confederation, something Tupper had always wanted. Thompson and Tupper were the Canadian commissioners to Washington in the fishery discussions, a prolonged and sometimes acrimonious negotiation with the Americans, but which finally resulted in a satisfactory treaty. Because he was again wearing two hats, this time the Minister of Finance, even though paid for only one, he was again criticized for holding two offices.

Some Conservative members were considering Tupper as the logical successor for Macdonald, and Macdonald agreed. Tupper, on the other hand disagreed when Macdonald raised the matter of succession with him, and said the position should go to Sir Hector Langevin, as had been previously agreed, since he was a French Canadian and Catholic, and the country would expect a rotation among the leadership. Macdonald said that if Tupper was to return to London as the High Commissioner, he would give his son, Charles Hibbert Tupper, a seat in the cabinet, which would please the father who saw his son as a future prime minister.

Back in London, Tupper worked on the financing for a line of steamships between Vancouver and China and Japan, the development of the rapid Atlantic steamship service and the continuing financial needs of the CPR. For his work in Washington on behalf of the fishery treaty he received a baronetcy from the Queen on the recommendation of the Imperial Government.

Tupper was a man of vision, but one of his reasonable suggestions again landed him in hot water. At a dinner given by members of the Imperial Federation League, he commented that little would come from their organization's efforts as long as they pursued the concept of a legislative federation that would render the various colonies of Britian subservient to the government in London. He could see, on the other hand, a federation of equal autonomous colonies, with representatives negotiating, as equals with London, preferential trade relationships (as occurred later in the British Commonwealth). The speech was received poorly by the host for the evening, Lord Herschell, and at home when it was reported in the Canadian newspapers. Sir John A. asked him to make it clear he was speaking as an individual, and not for the government, to which Tupper readily agreed.

Tupper continued to occupy himself in the role of statesman, which he enjoyed, although his masters at home often felt he acted too independently. He travelled on the continent, and although suffering an acute illness in Rome he was able to continue on to Florence where the Tuppers sat for their portraits by Professor Tito Conti.

On 21 January 1891 a cable arrived from Sir John A, Macdonald:

> Immediate dissolution almost certain. Your presence affect election contest in Maritime Provinces essential to encourage our friends. Please come. Answer.

Always ready to respond to a request from Macdonald, Tupper left for home and gave election speeches in communities all over Canada, travelling 3,722 miles. He was exhausted by the end of the campaign but when victory came many credited him with rescuing the tired government. Now Tupper and Macdonald knew all this was quite irregular. Despite the wrist slapping they had received on other occasions over the "two post" appointments, here they were at it again, with the High Commissioner, who should have been above and separate from party politics, out on the stump fighting for the government of the day led by his old party. Tupper's explanation, and he knew he had to produce one, was that the opposition was arguing for a policy of unrestricted trading reciprocity with the USA, which would eventually lead to Canada becoming part of that country. The future of the nation they had all worked so hard for was at risk, which justified his action. Or so he told many of his audiences. That didn't cut much ice with the defeated Liberals under Laurier. As soon as Tupper was back in London they raised the issue in the House, and Laurier entered a resolution criticizing Tupper's conduct as High Commissioner and his speeches that suggested the opposition was disloyal and treasonable in supporting reciprocity with the USA. The motion was defeated.

Word came that Sir John A. Macdonald was ill. Soon an unofficial telegram came from some cabinet members asking if Tupper would accept the nomination for Macdonald's seat in Kingston if he should die. Tupper's curt response was: "Thanks. Have no intention of re-entering Parliament."

Hibbert sent his father a coded telegram saying that there seemed to be a cabal against Tupper as a successor and in favor of Sir John Thompson. Hibbert said he would resign if Thompson were elected, but his father replied that he should support Thompson as nothing would induce him to return. Macdonald died of a stroke on 6 June 1891, but Thompson declined in favour of Senator John Abbott, who then became Prime Minister of Canada.

In the meantime, Tupper continued to speak on his concept for a federation of autonomous colonies, and wrote an article on the subject. It gained the approval of the Council of the Imperial Federation League, but his suggestion for a conference to pursue the idea was deferred. He didn't give up but answered the critics of his earlier paper by a second article. After a long and often heated public and private debate, Tupper held to his views while the federation waffled and finally dissolved.

Chapter 7 – Notes

1. George W. Ross; *Getting into Parliament and After.* Toronto: William Briggs. 1913.

2. Osler had three influential teachers, Rev. W.A. Johnson, who introduced him to the microscope and biology, Dr. James Bovell, who insired him towards medicine, and R. Palmer Howard, a great clinician and teacher. The R. Palmer Howard who writes about Osler (*The Chief: Doctor William Osler*; Caton, Mass. Science History Publications, 1983) is a grandson.

3. Daniel MacNeill Parker had made the same comment about the dangers of physicians serving two masters when he gave his acceptance speech as President of the Canadian Medical Association, succeeding Tupper, in 1870.

4. Cushing, Harvey; *The Life of Sir William Osler.* Oxford: Clarendon Press, 1925.

5. Between 1758 and 1992 there have been 66 physicians in Nova Scotia politics, the first being Dr. John Steele, an army surgeon elected in 1761, the latest being Premier John Savage MD, Minister of Health Ronald Stewart MD, Minister of Social Services James Smith MD, and Leader of the Opposition John Hamm MD, all serving in 1996. Most of the 66 physicians were Liberals (Liberals 45%, Conservatives 8%, Liberal Conservatives 15%, Progressive Conservatives 17%, and Reform 2%). Although

the names changed, 79% are of a liberal stripe. (The authors are grateful to Owen McInerney for this information). Tupper was a Conservative member, but liberal in his politics and beliefs.

6. Tupper's anxiety was justified as George Etienne Cartier, his colleague, died of Bright's disease, shortly after going down to defeat in 1873. Cartier was identified as the major figure in the Pacific Scandals.

7. Sir Andrew Clarke was born in Aberdeen in 1826, and overlapped with Tupper at Edinburgh medical school in 1842 and 1843, so they knew each other. Clarke was one of the most prominent English physicians, six times President of the Royal College of Physicians. His portrait, painted by Watts, who was also his patient, hangs in the Royal College in London. Clarke was an energetic, some said histrionic, physician who impressed his patients with his mixture of kindness, sermonizing and dogmatic instructions.

8. In his lecture, *An Enemy Of The Race*, on the scourge of alcohol, Sir Andrew said he saw ten thousand people per year and always inquired into their health habits. I calculate that 40 patients a day (an amazing number, if true), would certainly make him very rich. He said that 70% of people in hospital were there due to alcohol abuse. It was such a curse that he felt like giving up the profession and taking up a crusade to preach to all men: "Beware this enemy of the race."

9. Dr. Daniel MacNeill Parker also consulted Osler (1895) and Macdonald consulted Sir Andrew Clarke.

CHAPTER 9

On Guard For Thee

*"I can assure you that it is a source of great satisfaction
to me to know that you are with us amidst our political troubles,
and I feel assured that everyone will welcome you back again,
as we believe you can be of better service in guiding the ship of
state than any other man in the Dominion."*

H. A. Massey

7 January 1896

Tupper was now settled in to the life of a statesman in London and never expected to see the political stage again. In fact his only political aspiration was now to see his son as the Premier of Canada.

Always alert to any slight to Canadians by the British government, he successfully argued that it was inappropriate to ignore the title of Honorary for a Canadian minister or member of the Privy Council who moved to England. Next, he noted that a Bill was to be passed that would allow the collecting of death duties on properties in the colonies by those who moved to England. Again he was successful in having the bill amended so that only the difference between the higher death duty in Britain and the lower duty in Canada could be taxed in Britain. He urged the Imperial government to join Canada and Australia in connecting a Pacific cable between the two. In this, and in the crisis concerning the importation of live Canadian cattle into Britain, he was joined in the arguments and negotiations by Sir John Thompson. They worked together in mutual friendship and in common loyalty to Canada. While he was preparing to dine with the Queen at Windsor Castle, Tupper received word that Thompson had died suddenly. Tupper prepared to accompany the body back to Halifax, but Dr. Tyrrell and Dr. Travers pronounced his heart so "seriously affected" that they not only cancelled his plans to travel but ordered him to bed. It was two months before he could resume his duties.

At about this time, Tupper became involved in an attempt by the Fishmongers Company to block shipments of British Columbia salmon, arguing that they were trout, and therefore prohibited during the closed season for that fish. Two of the salmon had been offered to Tupper as a gift, so he knew this to be a ruse, and he devised one of his own. He asked the importer to send him another salmon, and sent it as a gift to the Director of the Natural History Museum and his wife. When Tupper went to see the Company officials to reverse the prohibition, he was told they could do nothing, as trout were illegal out of season. Tupper then presented the thank-you letter from the eminent scientist thanking him for the delicious "fine salmon", and the injunction was withdrawn.

A Call From Home

In the meantime changes were occurring at home. Bowell had become Premier of Canada (1894-1896) and Laurier was the formidable leader of the opposition. When the cabinet began to feel the need for a stronger leader, some considered the ageing and ailing Tupper in London. Tupper wrote to his son Charles Hibbert, saying he felt he would be the better leader, and that it would be a death sentence for Sir Charles himself to accept the leadership. He cautiously indicated that he might accept a seat in the Senate and in the government since he had been approached with the offer. He said he had no further personal ambitions as he had achieved all he had desired; he lived only for his wife and his children, and them alone. In truth, he lived a good life in London and saw little reason to change.

Despite all of these objections, Tupper was repeatedly encouraged to re-enter politics by his son, Charles Hibbert, who implored him to return, commenting that those outside cabinet and the *best* in cabinet were for him as leader. The best in cabinet might be for him, but others were definitely not in favour of the old warhorse's return. As always, he had plenty of enemies in Ottawa, chief among them the Governor General, Lord Aberdeen, and his wife Ishbel, who despised the older Tupper. Lord and Lady Aberdeen were Gladstone liberals, and Lady Aberdeen in particular was given to supporting liberal causes, such as the Rescue Mission, which rescued prostitutes from the Strand in London, and the League for the Provision of Seats for Shop Assistants. In Canada she had championed the National Council of Women, and in 1897 founded the Victorian Order of Nurses, which many doctors, including Tupper, opposed.[1]

Tupper was aware of the extent of his unpopularity at home, and saw very little reason to leave the happy life he and Frances had built for themselves in London only to return to the aggravation of parliamentary life in Ottawa. He responded to his son saying that it might be better for his son's fortunes if the party did lose and go into to opposition, as there Charles Hibbert could show his true mettle, and one day assume first the leadership and then the premiership.

Tupper was not willing to leave London for another reason. There he could more effectively fight for the fast Atlantic steamship service, for close commercial relationships with the other countries and colonies within the British Empire, and to prevent Newfoundland drifting commercially and perhaps politically towards the United States. He worried that if he moved to the Senate and back into politics these important issues would fail. If he could continue to press for Canada's interest in these matters and at the same time work to put his son in the line for the leadership, he might consider the Senate.

But this was not to be. The Manitoba school issue had returned to the political scene and his son had tendered his resignation over it. He later agreed to stay on, which made his father happy, although his unyielding stance on behalf of the Catholics and the rights for education were unchanged.

On 29 January 1895 the Judicial Committee of the Privy Council handed down its decision on the Manitoba schools question, by which it ruled that Roman Catholics had the right to separate schools in the Province of Manitoba, and as this right was denied them by the government of that province, an appeal to the Government of Canada according to the British North America Act could be entered, and the Parliament of Canada could enact and administer remedial legislation for Roman Catholics. Sir Charles agreed with the decision and said so in correspondence with Hibbert, but at that point he was ill in London and not directly involved in the discussions.

In December 1895 Tupper returned to Ottawa, and dined with the Premier, Sir Mackenzie Bowell. He outlined the success to date with the fast steamship service and the Pacific cable, and requested a peerage for Sir Donald Smith for his work on the CPR.

Some weeks later seven ministers tendered their resignations and came to Tupper to persuade him to seek the leadership. Tupper said he was in Ottawa at the request of Bowell, and would therefore accept no such support unless it came from Bowell. Days later Bowell sent for him and said he would resign in favour of Sir Charles. Tupper responded that he would have nothing to do with the party if they didn't put aside their bickering and unite behind him to do what must be done.

When word got out that Tupper might be brought back to lead the party, there was general approval even though some had serious reservations about having the "fighting doctor" back in their midst. There was concern that the old guard, and especially Tupper, carried too much baggage from the past, too much enmity from too many quarters. Others were reassured but concerned that his health and stamina might not be up to the challenge. They encouraged him to return but to bring energetic young politicians into the fold to shoulder much of the work. His old friend Daniel MacNeill Parker wrote to him saying that he hoped he would not return to Parliament for the good of his health, and then, in a second letter following close on the first, pleaded that if he did run it should not be in Cape Breton, where he feared he might fail. Bowell agreed that Tupper should return as leader in the House of Commons and then succeed as Prime Minister.

Tupper's career then took another of its dramatic turns. At the age of 75 he returned to Canada to re-enter politics. He resigned his directorships, accepted the position of Secretary of State and began a hectic tour of the country, attracting large audiences everywhere he went. There was a generally favourable press response to the return of The Grand Old Man. On 23 January 1896 he was nominated in Cape Breton County, where he was to be confronted by a formidable opponent, George H. Murray.[2] On the fourth of February Tupper was elected and a week later he took his seat in the House.

He received more good news with the birth of a grandson, the child of Charles Hibbert and Janet Tupper. The boy was named Victor Gordon, the first name to commemorate his grandfather's victory at the polls, the second to honour Governor General Lord Aberdeen, whose family name was Gordon. Lady Aberdeen was his godmother, a strange choice, since neither she nor the Governor General had ever made any secret of their dislike of the older Tupper. The boy would be known as Gordie.

Back in the House, Tupper was once again in his element. The most pressing government business was the Manitoba schools question, which has been called "the most complex and far-reaching of Canada's several crises involving minority school rights."[3] In Nova Scotia, when Tupper had imposed free tax-supported schools on the people of the province, he had refused to provide government funding to Catholic or other private schools, but after some discussion he reached a suitable compromise with the Catholic Bishop of Halifax, which allowed only for Catholic input, Catholic teachers and for after-hours religious classes. As Leader of the House in Ottawa, however, he came down strongly on the side of minority rights, and in March 1896 introduced remedial legislation. Some thought this was a strange turnaround, and suggested that Tupper was being forced to defend a move which he didn't fully support in order to court Quebec voters. However, Tupper, though a Protestant and a son of the manse, had argued before for the rights of the Catholic minority and he now insisted that the action of the Manitoba government had been an intrusion on the rights of a minority who were both French and Catholic. Laurier, a French Catholic, stood up to say the Remedial Bill would probably not give any relief to the Catholics and would be a "violent wrench of the constitution." Tupper, in his usual grandiloquent style responded:

> I would a thousand times rather fall in defence of the
> admitted rights of a weak minority of a race and religion not
> my own, than ride roughshod into power over the ruins

of the Constitution of my country and the denial of the just claims of a minority of my own race and faith at the behest of a majority who were trampling their dearest rights under their feet.

The bill was defeated, and Laurier, supported by anti-French and anti-Catholic votes in the House, (members of the Orange Order, Tupper said), forced its withdrawal. The government had no choice but to go to the people.

Tupper Becomes Prime Minister

On 27 April 1896 Bowell's resignation was accepted by the Governor General and Tupper, who had been asked to form the Government on the first of May started out on a whirlwind tour of towns and cities, giving two- to three-hour speeches each day. Despite his obvious vigour as he met his schedule of daily speeches throughout the country, the opposition press continually criticized the move to bring back a tired old man. What Tupper had not calculated, especially as it was the Conservative government which had defended the rights of the French Catholics, was that the Catholics in Quebec would still support Laurier and the Liberals. Ontario was evenly divided; all other provinces except Quebec gave a majority to the Conservatives. Forty-nine out of Quebec's 65 seats went to the Liberals, enough to tip the balance and defeat the Conservatives and the Grand Old Man.

It was a good fight. Tupper had unified and strengthened a weak, disorganized government, but was defeated by the unexpected support in Quebec for a French leader, even one who waffled on the rights of Catholics. "In modern Quebec, the Manitoba Schools Question is viewed as Canada's most significant loss of French and Catholic rights outside Quebec."[4]

Other bitter blows were to come. On election day he was informed of the death of his old friend and political ally, Sir Leonard Tilley, Lieutenant-Governor of New Brunswick. He was also shocked and angered when meeting with the Governor General to find that Aberdeen would not endorse the order-in-council to award the contract for the fast steamship service to Allans of Glasgow, even though it had already been passed by a unanimous vote of Parliament. He also found that the Governor General would not approve many of the appointments of the outgoing government even though this was Imperial practice and Canadian practice. Tupper, with justification, later angrily charged that the Governor General was acting politically. How much of a role Lady Aberdeen played in her husband's continuing rebuffs of Tupper is a matter for speculation. She had, after all, promised Annie Thompson that she would never see Tupper as leader of the party.

Tupper then put out a call for his parliamentary party members to meet and select a leader; he was unanimously elected. He and Frances were celebrating their golden wedding anniversary, enjoying congratulations and gifts from friends and colleagues all over the world. Lord and Lady Aberdeen joined in congratulating the couple by sending a gold gift box. Tupper, in returning the box to them, wrote to say that even if his Lordship had not previously announced the gift in the press, he would have returned it when it first arrived. As Leader of the Opposition, and an acknowledged leader in organized medicine, he would have another opportunity to repay earlier rebuffs by the Aberdeens by his opposition to Lady Aberdeen's Victorian Order of Nurses.

Over the next few years he showed great energy in opposition, defending the issues he felt were important for Canada, and arguing that Newfoundland should become part of Canada, and that Yukon should be represented in the House of Commons.

In 1899, he and Frances were both injured in a winter accident crossing the Saskatchewan River at Strathcona. Their sleigh capsized, and they were both thrown out onto the ice. Frances was the more seriously injured of the two, and Charles feared for her sight. He seriously injured his knee, and from then on had to contend with pain and some difficulty walking. He had to refuse an invitation to visit Prince Albert – he said he was "obliged to remain lying down with a view to getting into proper shape by the opening of Parliament." When he had nearly recovered he slipped on stairs and twisted the leg again while on a speaking engagement in his home town of Amherst. He spoke for an hour but later, speaking in Halifax, he was on crutches. In 1900 he stumped the country in preparation for the election, but spent little time in his Cape Breton constituency. The Conservatives were again defeated and Tupper lost his seat. There were regrets from many and offers for a safe seat elsewhere. He said he was relieved and would not consider again being pulled back into political life.

He did not go altogether graciously. In a letter to his constituents he complained he was defeated by "means of unfair voters' lists, many ignorant and partisan deputy returning officers, the illegal expenditure of public money during the campaign, not to mention many other unscrupulous acts on the part of government." He went on to say that Laurier owed his victory to the simple fact that he was French, and had appealed to Quebec on that basis, not that he was Canadian. He would later have the bittersweet satisfaction of seeing the Laurier government support virtually all the issues for which he had worked so hard.

His leave-taking from public life in 1900 was more graceful. He supported Borden as his successor as party leader, and he and Frances quietly retired to Bexleyheath, Kent, near London. Their home was The Mount, a fine old mansion near his daughter Emma and her family, overlooking a beautiful golf course where he would play until into his nineties. The view from The Mount was magnificent, and the town was near enough to London for them to keep in touch with their friends from his days as High Commissioner. His energy was still impressive, and over the next eight years he crossed the Atlantic 16 times. On one of these trips, being out of touch with the rapid changes on the stockmarket, he had lost $200,000 by the time he made shore. He was philosophical about it and would tell the story many times with gusto. He continued to be active, writing letters to the Editor, to his family and friends, and he completed his memoirs.

Although he was Tupper's severest critic during his career, J. S. Williston, the editor of *The Globe* for many years, and later *Toronto News*, admitted the "bold constructive genius" of Tupper, sheepishly confessing that his repeated charge that Tupper had enriched himself at the public expense had no foundation. He wrote that although it was fashionable to criticize the old war horse, history would give him a great place in the story of Canada. Alas, his contributions are well documented, but usually overlooked, and he is not as well remembered as his political enemies, many of whom were lesser lights.

In conversation with Williston in 1903, Tupper inquired about the comment in the generally laudatory article that there were some faults in his career. Tupper wanted him to explain the faults, but Williston promised, reluctantly, that he would only do so in a letter. In it he said that Tupper had done great things, but had supported governments that often used bad methods, even if their policies were good. He was referring to the use of contracts as bribes to communities, and other corruptions that lowered the standard of public ethics and morals. Although these acts were often carried out by governments, constituencies and corporations under government contracts, he still held Tupper personally responsible to a great extent, as a leader who could have changed these things. Tupper answered the letter with a detailed explanation of every incident, showing that he was not personally incriminated in any of the events listed. But his arguments could not alter the charge that these things were going on, and Tupper, as a prominent leader, had to accept some responsibility.

At eighty-four Tupper decided to learn Italian, so he hired a teacher to instruct him and his granddaughter. Within weeks he was reading Italian well, and said he even began to dream in Italian. His father had been noted for his knowledge of languages. At an audience with the Pope in 1905 he surprised the Pontiff by responding in Italian.

The Tuppers travelled back to Canada frequently during their retirement years, dividing their time between both countries. He continued to follow politics closely, especially issues that involved Canada internationally, and wrote letters to the papers and to politicians about issues that excited him. Some of these were lengthy, hard-hitting, and strong on logic, acid-tongued and based on a long memory. He wrote on Empire, on tariffs, and on the development of Canada as a nation. He published open letters to Laurier, Borden and Fielding. He was still invited to speak at dinners, and never lost the talent for giving long, well organized speeches. Throughout his career, in four or five hour speeches, Tupper impressed even his enemies by never using a note.

In 1907 he received a gracious invitation from the people of Cumberland County to a reception to honour him, tendered by members from both political factions. It was fifty two years since he had stepped on the school house stage to make his first political speech. During the half century of politics he had made a name for himself as the fearless, fighting doctor who could pummel his political foes unmercifully. To have people from all political parties join to honour him for his contributions was particularly gratifying. He had delayed the visit because of Lady Tupper's ill health, but they were able to go together a few months later, and to travel to Vancouver to see their children and grandchildren.

In Vancouver he was interviewed by the *Daily Advertiser* when he showed his sharp and incisive command of political events in Canada and England. In fact, as soon as he was back in England he wrote to *The Times* to correct its views on the Canadian constitution, and published a number of letters to the editor in Canada and England about Canada's naval policy. He was now eighty-seven years old.

In 1908 he was made a member of the Privy Council. By now he had to rely on a walking stick much of the time, and feared he would need it for the ceremony. The Privy Council Office assured him, "The King says he hopes Sir C. Tupper will by all means bring his stick with him when he is sworn in as P.C."

At a dinner to commemorate the sealing of Confederation at the Westminister Palace Hotel 44 years before, Laurier paid tribute to Tupper and his role in Confederation. "I believe I speak my mind and speak fair judgment of my countrymen when I say that next to MacDonald the man who did the most to bring Canada into Confederation is the veteran statesman on my left, Sir Charles Tupper. Reviewing the events of those days, everyone must admit there was no man who gave more of his heart and soul to the task than the gentleman who was then Doctor Tupper."

Chapter 9 – Notes

1. In fact, there was a good deal of organized opposition to the VON, and much of it sprang from organized medicine such as the Ontario Medical Society. In their minutes for June 3, 1897, they agreed that "kindly motives" had initiated the movement, but concluded that "it would be neglecting a serious duty if it failed to express its most unqualified disapproval of the scheme, on account of the dangers which must necessarily follow to the public should such an Order be established." Many newspapers supported the doctors, and the opposition from the doctors, along with some nurses who were afraid that the Order would undercut both their professional

authority and their pay, discouraged the government, under Laurier, from supporting the establishing of the VON with a grant. The VON received its charter in 1898, when Tupper was the Leader of the Opposition. (See *The Victorian Order of Nurses for Canada's 50th Anniversary 1897-1947* by John Murray Gibbon, printed by Southam Press Montreal for the Victorian Order of Nurses, 1947, and *Emily Stowe: Doctor and Suffragist* by Mary Beacock Fryer, Canadian Medical Lives no. 6, Toronto, Dundurn Press Ltd. 1990. pp. 116-118.)

2. George Murray would later be the longest serving Premier of Nova Scotia.

3. Paul Crunican in *The Canadian Encyclopedia*, Hurtig Publishers Ltd.; Edmonton; 1985; p. 1084.

4. Ibid.

CHAPTER 10

Envoi

Few men have lived more vigorously, first in the rough and tumble of a large general practice in Nova Scotia and then in a more turbulent area of politics, yet he retained good health of mind and body nearly to the end.

Sir William Osler

Individuals of moderate talents and influence drop out of the larger social circle when they retire, but not so Tupper. His biographer E. M. Saunders noted that he lived a whirlwind life decades after normal retirement age. In 1909, at the age of 89, he was enjoying dining in London with friends, spending time with grandchildren and playing golf on the course beside The Manor at Bexleyheath. He attended some meetings and conferences, but was beginning to act as if he were retired. He still followed politics closely, and had not lost his fighting spirit.

His lashing out at the Honourable W. S. Fielding, Premier of Nova Scotia, in a long letter to the *Toronto News*, when he was ninety, showed every bit of his punchy style and hard-hitting logic. [1] When Fielding tried to respond, Tupper lashed out again in a long, detailed outline of Fielding's misrepresentation of the Washington negotiations over reciprocity and other events back to 1868, indicating that Fielding really deserved "little notice at my hands" because his response did not refute any of Tupper's arguments. That didn't stop Tupper from again pounding Fielding on every point. If there was any doubt why Tupper was called the Fighting Doctor, one need only read this newspaper debate when he was ninety years old!

His spirit was strong, but his health was failing. After a speech at the Westminster Hotel, commemorating the Confederation event in those rooms fifty years before, he sighed, "My speaking days are done." This wasn't quite true as he accepted an invitation to address the United Empire Club in London at a luncheon in his honour (he felt he wasn't up to the formal dinner originally planned). The *Canadian Gazette* reported, "Sir Charles Tupper then paid one of his now all-too-rare visits to London to be the guest of the club at luncheon, and made a speech which, by its vigour and lucidity and patriotic fervour, happily belied the tale of years recorded against the speaker. For thirty-five minutes he spoke without a note, with more than his accustomed command of expression and rhetoric, and without a hesitating word – a feat which, we fancy, has seldom been equaled by an octogenarian."

Saunders comments that although his intellect was as keen as ever and his interest "in his beloved Canada abated not one jot," he was now awaiting the "closing in of the twilight."

In the winter of 1911-1912 he had a severe bout of bronchitis and his physicians feared he would not recover. At the same time Frances's health began to fail. Tupper was making daily brief diary notes of his worries about her health, and the comments of Mr. Tyrell and Sir Charles Kennedy who provided regular medical attention for her. On 13 May 1912 she died at the age of 86.

Charles and Frances had been through a lot in their sixty-six years together. She had married an up and coming country doctor, and they had made a home in a small provincial town, but soon she found herself part of a much larger, much more dramatic event, the birth of a country. The early years were not without sadness, as two of their young daughters died. As Tupper moved quickly from place to place, Frances often stayed behind, making a home for their children – William was only five years old at the time of Confederation in 1867. Wherever he settled, in Halifax, Ottawa, Toronto or London, they moved house, usually renting a suitable place. Their family time was often spent in the Maritimes at their summer home in St. Andrews, chosen both because of its beauty and because it was on the direct rail line from Montreal, and on an island near their first home in Amherst. As the children grew up Frances and Charles travelled together, and she was his companion on many of the trips throughout the country and across the Atlantic.

Tupper accompanied the body back to Halifax where burial took place at St. John's Cemetery, in the grave where their little daughters Lily and Sophie were also buried. Frances's death took the wind out of the old warrior's sails. After the funeral he made one last trip across his beloved Canada, stopping in Winnipeg and Vancouver to spend time with his children and grandchildren. His last visit was to Amherst, his home town, the place where he began as a country doctor and surgeon 68 years before. The town proclaimed a holiday in his honour, and two thousand people came out to greet him. They were impressed with what they saw – a man of 92 who was still strong, with good hearing and eyesight, strong voice, and a sharp and agile mind. The leonine features, the flashing eyes, the strong, determined chin had not changed. The Grand Old Man, the Warhorse of Cumberland, the Father of Confederation, was making his last public appearance in the place where it had all begun. He stayed for two days, then left for Saint John to sail for England.

His son Stewart came to visit him at Bexleyheath, and while there suffered what appears to have been a stroke. Sir William Osler helped to make the arrangements for Stewart to be cared for in a nursing home in Oxford and repeatedly visited and relayed reports to Tupper, but Stewart died in 1914.

Tupper was often depressed during these last years. He was very disturbed by the war, worrying about his grandsons at the front, and he was failing in health. [2] In his last year, 1915, he was frequently examined by Osler, often called in by Tupper's two physicians, the young local physician Dr. Thomas W. Hinds and the prominent Sir Douglas Powell. On many other occasions Osler visited socially as an old friend, sometimes accompanied by Lady Osler. In Tupper's daybooks there are notations of about 15 visits by Osler from 1913 to 1915. When Tupper was in Oxford or when Osler was in London, these visits were often made daily, and occasionally Lady Osler would visit alone when Sir William was unable to do so.

His son, Charles Hibbert, made some notes about the last period of his father's life. (Hibbert was receiving frequent letters from his sister Emma Cameron.) In April Sir Charles went to Oxford where he was examined by his old friend Osler, who said that the gradual deterioration of his health was just due to his age, and not to any specific illness. Emma said that Osler found his arteries "wonderful" for a man of his years, his pulse good and his strength considerable.

On the 12th of July in 1915, he consulted Sir Douglas Powell in London. He was suffering from what he called bronchial irritation. On the 22nd of September he had a heart attack. Dr. Hinds prescribed rest, and he seemed to recover, but on the 26th of October the doctor was sent for again. This time he brought Sir William Osler with him. Tupper had been laid up in his room for three weeks and seemed quite depressed. At night he had vivid dreams about his "darling Frances," which he described in his diary each day. He worried about his grandson Reggie who had been severely injured in battle; he was being shipped back home across the Atlantic. Emma said he was constantly thinking about Reggie and "he is glad to think he is such a good man as well as a brave one." A few days later, on October 29, he went to bed and died that night in his sleep.

Although the son of a Baptist minister, Sir Charles inclined to the Anglican faith, attending the parish church in Bexley. It was natural that his funeral service should be held there. The vicar spoke of Tupper as "Canada's Grand Old Man, to whose . . . wise counsels and unselfish and unceasing labour the British Empire owes so much." He said "the name of Sir Charles Tupper will be gratefully associated with the Dominion as long as that Anglo-Saxon nation exists. . . . He was undeniably one of the greatest, if not the greatest of our empire builders, a statesman of the first rank. . . . Duty was his watchword, devotion to duty a leading feature of his noble character, a far-seeing man of clear vision and broad and liberal views, of conspicuous ability, of cultured mind and generous heart and hand, the soul of honour, a very perfect gentleman."

A memorial service was also held at St. Margaret's, Westminster, attended by dignitaries and friends from London, including representatives of the Crown and the Colonial Office, members of the High Commission staff in London, and a large number of Canadians who were living in England, including Sir William Osler. His body was taken on board the warship HMS *Metagma*, for one last transatlantic crossing. The ship arrived in Quebec, and the last part of his journey home to Halifax was, fittingly, by train.

He was given a state funeral in Halifax on a clear, sunny 16th of November. The funeral cortege walked from the venerable old St. Paul's on the Grand Parade to St. John's Cemetery, where, with full state honours, he was laid to rest beside Frances.[3]

The Obituary

As a mark of their friendship, Sir William Osler was asked by the major journals to write the obituary notice, and his account of Tupper's life was used in the *Lancet*, the *British Medical Journal* and the *Canadian Medical Journal* (the full obituary can be found in Appendix 2).

Osler wrote, "Few men have lived more vigorously, first in the rough and tumble of a large general practice in Nova Scotia and then in a more turbulent area of politics, yet he retained good health of mind and body nearly to the end."

Tupper never tired of talking of his happy days at Edinburgh and only months before his death Osler had encouraged him to write his experiences as a medical student. Osler talked about his founding of the Canadian Medical Association, and of his medical practices in Amherst, Halifax, Ottawa and Toronto:

> He was fond of surgery, and was one of the few men remaining who could talk of personal experiences in pre-anaesthetic days. He told the writer of an amputation at the hip joint for sarcoma performed on a farmer's wife on the kitchen table, with a sailor as assistant. The patient lived 18 miles away, so he was never able to make a second visit. Three months later the farmer drove to Amherst with his wife strong and well. Canada owes a deep debt to Sir Charles Tupper, and his political opponent, Sir Wilfred Laurier, very truly said that next to Sir John A. MacDonald, the man who did most to bring about the federation of the Canadian provinces was Sir Charles Tupper. With a strong and daring personality, he had all the qualities for success in the public life – calmness and clear judgement in victory, resolution and hopefulness in defeat. Nothing in his history was more remarkable than to

have "stumped the country" successfully for his party when in his 80th year.

His life is an illustration of the brilliant success of the doctor in politics. We have to go to France or to the South American Republic to parallel his career. But, he never really served two masters; from 1855 he was a politician first, and practitioner only when stranded by the exigencies of party.

Osler comments that Tupper was alert and clear during his last few months, and his arteries were healthy and "scarcely palpable when the blood stream was pressed out." He concludes with the exclamation, "Yet here was a man who in 1880-1881 was ready to throw out the sponge, as he was believed to have Bright's disease!" He indicated that with his discovery that this type of renal condition was benign, Tupper lived another healthy 34 years. "The advantage of the discovery was never better illustrated, as he ever after lived a careful life."

Remembering Tupper

Condolences came to the family from friend and foe alike, all acknowledging his contributions, vision and tireless efforts for his country. R.L. Borden, then Prime Minister of Canada, said, "The greatest living Canadian passed away in him."

The Hon. T. Chase Casgrain K.C. wrote to his son in Ottawa:

Sir Charles Tupper was not only one of the builders of this country but a constant worker in maintaining the integrity of the structure which he helped to create. Interpreting the Canadian constitution as a promise and a bond of union between the different elements which go to make up the nation he courageously and at the cost of his popularity for the time being fought patriotically to have that constitution interpreted according to the spirit in which it was conceived and adopted by the imperial Parliament. In the history of Canada the name of Sir Charles Tupper will be given a foremost place as that of a broad-minded and liberal statesmen to whom posterity will do that justice which some of his compatriots refused him during his lifetime.

The Liberal press, which had given him such a hard ride during his career, even admitting they created many of the negative stories about him, expressed warm reminiscences about a politician and orator who was unlike any other. "He waited not for occasions, he made them," said the *Evening Mail*.

Messages came from his constituents and former patients, remembering some personal connection with the Grand Old Man. One letter from a conductor on the railway said Sir Charles was always a "great friend of the 'old boys' all over the Intercontinental Railway."

Chapter 10 – Notes

1. *Toronto News*, May 1, 1911. Also reported by Saunders, p. 267-275.

2. Reggie was wounded but was sent back home and lived. But Charlie's son, Captain Victor Gordon Tupper, died at Vimy Ridge and was buried in France. He was 21.

3. The grave is marked by a large, plain brown, marble gravestone, and nearby are additional stone markers, one from the government of Canada noting his many roles in the service of his country as a Father of Confederation and Prime Minister, and another from the Presidents of the Canadian Medical Association marking his role as the first President of the CMA and his three terms of office.

4. *Evening Mail*, November 1, 1915.

CHAPTER 11

Epilogue

In legislating for his country, Sir Charles's motto was
"Buy the Truth and sell it not."

E.M. Saunders D.D.

Hector Langevin had this recollection of two of his fellow Fathers of Confederation: "John A. Macdonald is a sharp fox . . . very well informed, ingratiating, clever, very popular. . . . Mr Tupper of Nova Scotia is capable but too incisive; he makes bitter enemies for himself; he is ambitious and a gambler."[1] Contemporary accounts of Tupper seem to bear out Langevin's judgment. Despite the major role he played in the development of Nova Scotia and Canada, current historians, particularly those who have written biographies on his "bitter enemies," choose to ignore his capabilities and his considerable accomplishments.

Sir John A. Macdonald was one who recognized Tupper's ability to go directly to the heart of the matter, an ability that had also stood him in good stead in his role as a physician. His willingness to gamble, even at the risk of making enemies, were qualities Macdonald and Canada needed: "Send Tupper" was the cry when action was required. Tupper was almost unfailingly loyal to Macdonald, and was willing to suffer the criticism and the animosity; the letters between the two men make clear Macdonald's dependence on him.

Sir John Willison, the newspaper editor, first of *The Globe*, and later the *Toronto News*, was one of Tupper's "bitter enemies." On Tupper's death he compared the two Fathers of Confederation. He said, "Sir Charles Tupper was pre-eminently a constructive statesman. He was deficient in the managing genius which Sir John A. Macdonald displayed during the infancy of Confederation. He drove; Macdonald led. He overcame by sheer force and courage; Macdonald by persuasion and attraction. He made sacrifices to conciliate Howe and reconcile the eastern provinces to Confederation." But he continued, "He was the driving force behind the construction of the Canadian Pacific Railway. . . . He more than any other man called Sir John Macdonald to keep his compact with the west." [2]

Later Sir John Willison wrote an article in the *Dalhousie Review* on Pope's "Life of Macdonald", and made this comment on the letters between Macdonald and Tupper: "Those that appear illustrate Macdonald's dependence upon Tupper in every crisis, show how Tupper reinforced the courage and restored the confidence of the leader, and afford additional evidence that bold, ambitious and dominant though Tupper was, he was not intractable and never failed to respond to any appeal for party or country. One wonders when history will adjust the balances. There is a glamour about Howe such as never has encompassed Tupper, although Tupper was the greater in force, in vision, in practical constructive genius, and in service to Canada and the Empire. He [Tupper] was inferior only in genius for agitation, in instinct for constitutional reform, and in the pomp and passion of oratory."

To Saunders, Tupper was one of the greatest non-professional journalists of his day, important in his writing up until his ninetieth year. His "lucid, nervous, vigorous style and his sensitively responsive memory" of events and their meaning continued to instruct the public long after he had officially retired from public life.

In Nova Scotia, politics are felt strongly and divisions can run deep. In the late nineteenth century you were either a Tupper man or a Howe man, and in the late twentieth century very little appears to have changed. Even those with only a passing knowledge of history speak of Howe in glowing terms, aware of his efforts for responsible government and freedom of the press, for which the adulation is well deserved. "Tupper? Well," they say, "there's a school named after him. And wasn't he the man who was Prime Minister of Canada for the shortest period of time?" Howe fans are adamant that ideas like free education and Confederation were originally his. There is no dispute that Howe tried to encourage free education, and inaugurated, for example, a Mechanics Institute to promote learning in Nova Scotia. He was, however, politically nervous in following through with the concept. Tupper was not. Howe was a man who needed the approbation of the public; he was afraid to go the last mile towards implementation lest he lose the approval of the adoring throngs. Whatever has been said about him unfavourably, no contemporary would have suggested that Tupper was afraid of anything or anyone, and "fearless" is used most often to describe him. Because he was willing to take the risk, all Nova Scotia children, not only the children of the rich, were given the opportunity to attend school.

It is also true that Howe spoke of the advantages of confederation, although he never appeared to embrace it fully, preferring a Nova Scotia that stood alone as part of the British Empire. When Tupper gave him the opportunity to take part in the Charlottetown meeting, even though he was no longer in government, Howe declined, citing a lack of time due to his role as Fisheries Commissioner; he nevertheless sent his blessing. When the representatives of the other provinces visited Halifax in August 1864, he spoke glowingly of the possibility of union. But later he asked, "Whoever heard of a public man being bound by a speech delivered on such an occasion as that?"[3]

Tupper, however, risked his reputation and his very life to bring the Maritime colonies into the union. His vision was of a strong country that stretched from sea to sea, British North America; a country too large and too strong to be swallowed up by the United States of America. It was Howe who fought against Confederation, calling it the Botheration Scheme. He had no interest in belonging to a federation that stretched "westward to the backwoods of Canada."[4] And, always the brilliant orator, he uttered the words that still stir the hearts of Nova Scotians: "Take a Nova Scotian to Ottawa, away above tidewater, freeze him up for five months, where he cannot view the Atlantic, smell salt water, or see the sail of a ship, and the man will pine and die."[5]

In his pamphlet "Joseph Howe – Anti-Confederate", J. Murray Beck muses that "just because Confederation appears to have been successful"[6] it doesn't necessarily mean that Tupper had the clearer vision, and took the correct stand. Since we count ourselves among those who still think Canada was a good idea, we prefer Tupper's vision, but we also understand the very real concerns of Howe and his followers. It is unfortunate that Nova Scotia has been unable or unwilling to recognize the strengths of each of these great men.[7] The sad concluding sentence in Hibbert Tupper's supplement to his father's "Recollections" reads, "The erection of a monument in the Parliament Square at Halifax is only retarded by the question of money." The monument was never erected, but Joseph Howe stands in the square, on a pedestal facing the harbour, his hand in the air, testing the wind.

There is a monument to Tupper, however, and it is perhaps more fitting. In 1967, when each province initiated a project which would commemorate the one hundredth anniversary of Confederation, Dr. Chester Stewart, Dean of the Faculty of Medicine, a keen student of history, encouraged the province of Nova Scotia to make their Centennial Project a new medical school building, named for Tupper. In the foyer of the main building, there's a bust of Sir Charles, looking stern and strong and incisive, and ready for a fight.

The question most often asked, when others heard that we were writing a biography of Tupper, was: Is it true he was a woman-izer? These were usually people who had read Heather Robertson's disappointing, inadequately researched chapter on Frances Tupper in "More Than A Rose." Ms Robertson seemed to think that anyone who travels a lot must have many mistresses, and pictured poor Lady Tupper tucked away somewhere while her husband wandered off to Toronto. As it happened, Tupper and his wife wandered off to Toronto together in 1876. He set up a medical practice there, when their daughter-in-law, Stewart's wife, Mary Wilson Robertson, died in childbirth leaving a baby girl, Marie Stewart Tupper. The senior Tuppers became close guardians of their motherless granddaughter, and she was with them for many years until they died in England. Some castigated Tupper for consorting with women other than his wife,[8] others rebuked him for nepotism, for acting too quickly and too forcefully on behalf of his children, seeking army promotions for his son-in-law and political roles for his sons. Not enough of a family man? Too much of a family man? Take your pick. Like Joseph Howe, he enjoyed the company of attractive women and many of them enjoyed his company. Some, on the other hand, disliked him, notably Ishbel Gordon, Lady Aberdeen, and Thompson's wife, Annie.

There was another outstanding statesman-physician born the same year as Tupper, the Berlin pathologist Rudolf Virchow. Virchow became a member of the Prussian parliament, and a powerful opponent of German totalitarianism. His violent opposition to Bismarck led to Bismarck's challenge to a duel. But Virchow is best remembered for his expressed belief that "medicine is a social science, and politics nothing else but medicine on a large scale,"[9] a belief shared by Tupper and his Edinburgh professors.

Tupper was always a doctor, and was willing to give medical help and attention whenever he could. And he was by all accounts a good doctor. Certainly, Edinburgh provided him with an excellent medical education, as well as the opportunity to associate with some of the outstanding physicians of the time. He was hard-working and much in demand. He had a reputation for being a good physician and surgeon, as noted by Osler, and he always was able to build a good practice when the interests of his political career or the needs of his family dictated a move to another city. He also had a broad vision of medicine and the health of the people, just as he had broad visions in politics, arguing for a national medical association, a Maritime medical school, an office of statistics, better care for the poor, better hospital services and the importance of public health. His son recalled an incident in Halifax in which rioters at a meeting harassed all the speakers except Tupper. When his son asked why this was, he was told that they respected Tupper because he never refused to go on a house call.

Most of all though, Tupper was a patriot. He knew the country from sea to sea, and he loved it. A Nova Scotian by birth, he had lived in New Brunswick as a child, and later had a summer practice in an exquisite home in St. Andrews, New Brunswick. He spent many of his political years in Ottawa, but lived also in Toronto, where his eldest son lived, and he knew Quebec and Ontario equally well. He spent time in Manitoba, where his youngest son, William, later became Lieutenant-Governor, and he followed the railway through the west until the last spike was driven. His second son, Charles Hibbert, became a Cabinet Minister, and lived in British Columbia, where Tupper often visited him.

After his death, a Victoria paper wrote:

Sir Charles Tupper typified in a higher degree than any other man of his time the true Canadian spirit. Aggressive, alert, forceful, far-seeing, he hewed his own career through a forest of giants, and well typified the same struggle of his country through all the early stages of nationhood. Sir Charles Tupper reached the summit of his ambition and lived to see the country he loved so well realize that national status which was always his fondest dream. . . . Meanwhile Canada recognizes the loss of one whom she can scarcely mourn because of the ripe-ness of his age, the fullness of his service and the perpetu-ation of his invincible spirit in the national life.

When will history adjust the balance?

In this record of Canada's great statesman, one feature of his character stands out pre-eminently – his courageous optimism – an optimism conditioned on knowledge and valiant contention for truth, but at the same time an optimism which made full allowance for the strength and number of the forces opposed to him. It did not beget care-lessness or inaction. To him success was the reward of battles intelligently and courageously fought against what he considered unsound principles and politics. He ever saw the banner of victory waving and heard the shouts of the victors. This unfailing optimism ever strengthened his heart, and in all circumstances made for him a bright future. To him defeat was not defeat. It was a mere accident to be neutralised preparatory to genuine success.

E.M. Saunders D.D.

Chapter 11 – Notes

1. Quoted in Newman, Lena. *The John A Macdonald Album*. Montreal, Tundra Books of Montreal. 1974, p. 67.

2. Tupper, Sir Charles Hibbert. *Supplement to the Life and Letters of the Rt. Hon. Sir Charles Tupper, Bart., GCMG*. Toronto. The Ryerson Press. 1926, pp. 188, 189.

3. Quoted by J. Murray Beck in *Joseph Howe Anti-Confederate* Historical Booklet # 17 in the Canadian Historical Association series.

4. Ibid p. 15.

5. Ibid p. 15.

6. Ibid p. 18.

7. The computer index in the Halifax Library lists twenty-six entries under Howe, two under Tupper.

8. Waite, Peter B., *The Man From Halifax: Sir John Thompson, Prime Minister*. Toronto. University of Toronto Press. 1985.

9. Ackerknecht, Erwin H., *Rudolf Virchow: Doctor, Statesman, Anthropologist*. Madison. The University of Wisconsin Press. 1953. p. 48.

10. Tupper, Sir Charles Hibbert. *Supplement to the Life and Letters of the Rt. Hon. Sir Charles Tupper, Bart., GCMG*. Toronto. The Ryerson Press. 1926, p. 193.

Appendices

Sir Charles Tupper.
A Genealogy and Chronology

1522   Tupper family, then known as Topfer, in Hesse-Cassel.

1578, Jan 28   Thomas Tupper born in Bury, Sussex, England.

1637   Thomas Tupper to Sandwich, Mass., marries
                daughter of Governor Mayhew of Massachusetts.

1711, June 20   Thomas Tupper's great-grandson, Eliakim Tupper Jr.,
                born in Sandwich, Mass..

1761   Eliakim's family to Cornwallis, Nova Scotia, as New
                England Planters.

1794, Aug 6   Eliakim's great-grandson, Charles, born in
                Aylesford, Nova Scotia.

1818, Dec   Rev. Charles, who had become a Baptist minister,
                marries Miriam (Lockhart) Lowe, and moves to
                Amherst, Nova Scotia.

1821, July 2   Charles Tupper born.

1823   Nathan Tupper, Charles's brother, born in Amherst.

1829, Aug 27   Charlotte Tupper, Charles's sister, born in Amherst.

A Chronology

1836	At the age of 15, Charles leaves school to apprentice in medicine with Dr. Benjamin Page in Amherst.
1837, Aug	Studies at Horton Academy. His friendship with Daniel MacNeill Parker begins.
1839, Nov	Apprenticed to Dr. E.B. Harding, in Windsor, November 1839 to August 1840.
1840	Leaves Canada for medical study in Edinburgh.
1843, April	Graduates from Edinburgh University Medical School.
	Returns to Amherst to establish a large country medical and surgical practice.
1846, Oct	Marries Frances Amelia Morse of Amherst.
1847, July	Daughter Emma born.
Sept	Nathan Tupper marries Eleanor Bent.
1849, April	Second daughter Lily born. She dies the following year.
1851, July	Tupper's mother dies.
1851, Oct	Son, James Stewart, born.
1852, March	Tupper invited to introduce J.W. Johnstone at a Conservative meeting, and has his first run-in with Joseph Howe. This was the beginning of his life in politics.
1855, May 22	Tupper defeats Joseph Howe in an election.
1855, Aug	Second son, Charles Hibbert born.
1856	Howe regains seat in the provincial legislature representing Hants County; his anti-Catholic rhetoric contributes to the downfall of the Young government.

1857	Johnstone and the Conservatives form the government with Johnstone as Premier and Tupper as Provincial Secretary.
1858, Feb 28	Daughter, Sophie Almon Tupper, born.
	Tupper goes to England with W.A. Henry and R.B. Dickey of Nova Scotia and Galt, Cartier and Rose of Canada to discuss the proposed Intercolonial Railway.
1859	In the election Tupper keeps his seat but the Conservatives defeated. Young was Premier without ministry, Howe Provincial Secretary.
1860	Chief Justice Halliburton dies. Young appointed to the post, Howe becomes Premier. Tupper moves to Halifax to take his seat, and has a lucrative medical practice. Appointed City Medical Officer. Editor of the *British Colonist*.
	During the life of the government he keeps up a barrage of attacks against Howe and his party.
	Tupper gives lecture on "The Political Condition of British North America" on the occasion of the opening of the Mechanics' Institute in Saint John, New Brunswick.
1862, June 29	Youngest son, William Johnston, born at Halifax.
	Tupper, Joseph Howe, William Young and S.L. Shannon named first provisional governors of Dalhousie College.
1863, May	Election, dominated by Tupper, results in a crushing defeat for Howe and the Liberals. Johnstone becomes premier for a short time.
Aug 13	Daughter Sophie, dies of diphtheria, age five.
Nov	Introduces resolution at Dalhousie to found a medical school.

1864	Johnstone given seat on the Bench. Tupper, age 43, becomes Premier of Nova Scotia.
1864	Tupper successfully defeats motion to close down Dalhousie College.
	Tupper convenes meeting in Charlottetown to discuss Maritime Union. Representatives from Canada attend. The group became known as the Fathers of Confederation.
	In addition to Tupper, Nova Scotia delegates include: Attorney-General William Henry, the Hon. R.B. Dickey of Amherst, Liberal leader the Hon. Adams Archibald and the Hon. Jonathon McCully, a former teacher of Tupper, leader of the Liberals in the Legislative Council. Joseph Howe and John Locke of Shelburne decline invitation to attend.
Oct 10	Conference to discuss union of all the provinces held in Quebec.
1865	Premier Tupper introduces and pushes through Act of Education, which provides Nova Scotia with British North America's first system of free, non-sectarian schools, supported by direct taxation.
1866, Apr 10	Tupper moves confederation resolution in Nova Scotia House.
Apr 14	Fenian Raids in New Brunswick.
Apr 18	Confederation vote taken in Nova Scotia House. 31 to 19 in favour.
1867, July 1	British North America Act proclaimed, combining Ontario, Quebec, Nova Scotia and New Brunswick into one country – Canada.
1867	Companion of the Bath (CB) awarded.
1867-1875	William Annand anti-confederate (Liberal) Premier of Nova Scotia.

1867, Nov 6	First meeting of the Dominion Parliament in Ottawa (moved from Halifax).
1867	Tupper elected founding President of the Canadian Medical Association (CMA).
1868, Feb	Joseph Howe and anti-confederates go to London to build support in Westminister for their cause. Tupper follows. Tupper and Howe meet in London. Tupper persuades Howe to change his mind.
June 17	British Government refuses request of anti-confederates.
Sept	Howe accepts a seat in the Dominion Government, runs and wins in Hants County.
1869, Apr	Tupper and Howe travel to Ottawa with the Nova Scotia delegation.
Feb	Medical Faculty approved at Dalhousie.
Mar	Tupper declines chairmanship of Intercolonial Railway Commission.
1868-1870	Tupper resumes his medical practice at Ottawa.
1868, Sept	Elected President of CMA for second term.
1869, July	Daughter Emma marries Captain D.R. Cameron of the Royal Artillery. Posted to Fort Garry.
Sept	Elected CMA President for third term.
Dec 3	Leaves for Fort Garry at his wife's request to look for Emma.
	Tupper meets with Riel at Fort Garry, becomes friends with Sister Riel, Louis Riel's sister, and Sister MacGregor. The friendships last for their lifetimes.
1870	Manitoba enters Confederation.
July	Dalhousie Medical School expanded from two year program to a full four year MDCM program.

1871	Tupper President of Council of Dominion cabinet.
	British Columbia enters Confederation.
1872	Tupper Minister of Inland Revenue.
1873	Tupper Minister of Customs.
	Prince Edward Island joins Confederation.
	Howe appointed Lieutenant-Governor of N.S.; dies June 1.
	Conservative government defeated.
	Dr. Tupper continues medical practice in Ottawa in winter and in St. Andrews, New Brunswick, in summer.
1875, Sept	James Stewart Tupper marries Mary Wilson Robertson.
1876, Aug	Mary dies giving birth to Marie Stewart Tupper. Marie survives and becomes favourite of her Tupper grandparents.
	Charles and Frances move to Toronto to assist in her care.
	The Herald begins publishing in Nova Scotia.
1878, Sept	Conservatives return to power. Tupper Minister of Public Works. He and Frances return to Ottawa.
1879	National Policy implemented: tariffs raised from 17% to over 30%.
	Tupper Minister of Railways.
May 10	Tupper presents a resolution in the House proposing the Canadian Pacific Railway.
May 24	Her Majesty the Queen confers knighthood on Tupper (KCMG).
Sept	Charles Hibbert Tupper marries Janet MacDonald.
1880, Dec 10	Hibbert and Janet have a son, Charles.

1880-81	Tupper believed to have Bright's disease. Referred to Sir William Osler.
1881, Jan 19	Tupper's father, the Rev. Charles Tupper, dies at Kingston, Nova Scotia.
1882, June	Federal election won by the Conservatives. Sir Charles elected in Cumberland by acclamation; son Charles Hibbert elected for the first time in Pictou.
	Sir Charles ill. Goes to England with Sir William Osler to consult Sir Andrew Clark; then to Ireland for rest.
May	Hibbert and Janet have a daughter, Sophie Almon.
1883	Sir Charles appointed High Commissioner to United Kingdom.
	Continues as Minister of Railways.
Sept	Tupper persuades U.K. government to reverse ban on Canadian cattle after performing autopsy.
	Fielding liberal Premier of N.S.
1884, April	Fight in cabinet between Tupper and Macdonald over continuation of the railway from Truro to Sydney. The friendship between the two permanently strained.
May 28	Tupper resigns from Canadian parliamentary life, returns to England to continue as High Commissioner.
June 17	Tuppers take up residence at 97 Cromwell Road in London.
Aug 8	A son, Charles Stewart Tupper, born to J. Stewart Tupper and his second wife, the former Ada Galt, in London. Stewart and Ada also had two daughters.
1885, Jan	Hibbert and Janet have second daughter, Frances Lillian.
	The Northwest (Riel) Rebellion.

Nov 7	The last spike for the transcontinental railway driven by Donald Smith.
Nov 16	Louis Riel executed by hanging in Regina.
1886	Sir Charles decorated with GCMG. (Knight Grand Cross of St. Michael and St. George).
Sept	Dr. Nathan Tupper dies in Halifax.
1887, July 6	Tupper's son, William Johnston, marries Margaret MacDonald, Janet's sister. Later becomes Lieutenant-Governor of Manitoba.
Dec 22	Hibbert and Janet have a second son, James Macdonald.
1888	Sir Charles created a Baronet.
1889	Visits Canada with Lady Tupper, their daughter Emma Cameron and their granddaughter Sophie Cameron. They visit Kingston, Winnipeg, Pelican Lake, Toronto, Vancouver, Victoria, Esquimalt, Banff, Winnipeg again, and finally Montreal whence they sail to Liverpool.
June 22	Tupper suggests a Conference of all the autonomous British colonies to promote the unity of the Empire, including a policy of preferential trade.
1890	Tupper ill in London; seen by Dr. Charles, Lord Dufferin's physician.
	Princess Louise calls to check on his health.
Mar 30	His friend Andrew Robertson dies. Robertson was the father of Mary Robertson Tupper.
	Professor Tito Conti paints portraits of Sir Charles and Lady Tupper in Florence.
	Sir Charles meets Lord Rosebery to discuss Australian confederation.
1891, Oct 18	Hibbert and Janet have third daughter, Janet Miriam Grace (Holland).

Sir Charles returns to Canada to help
Sir John A. MacDonald with a federal election.
Works to the point of exhaustion, finally travelling
to Amherst where he rested for a few days.

Apr 15   Arrives in London.

June 6   Sir John A. MacDonald dies, replaced as
             Prime Minister by Senator Abbott.

Oct   Tupper again introduces the idea of a federation
             of the British Empire colonies.

July 15   Sophie Cameron, daughter of Emma, married
             C.H. Gray

1892, Apr 14 University of Edinburgh confers honorary LLD
             on Sir Charles.

Oct 12   Tupper attends Alfred Lord Tennyson's funeral
             at Westminster Abbey.

1893   Hibbert's and Janet's third son, Reginald Hibbert,
             born.

1894, Dec 12 Sir John Thompson dies in London. Tupper ordered
             to bed by Dr. Tyrrell and Dr. Travers for heart disease.

1895, Jan 29 Judicial Committee of the Privy Council passes
             decision on the Manitoba Schools question.
             Sir Charles, ill in London, agrees with the decision.

             Called back to Canada to help in the
             election campaign.

1896, Feb 4 Tupper elected in Cape Breton. Hibbert's and
             Janet's youngest child, Victor Gordon, born.

Feb 11   Tupper takes seat in the House.

Mar 3   Moves second reading of the Remedial Bill.

Mar 20   Remedial Bill carried.

Apr 23   Parliament prorogued; Sir MacKenzie Bowell
             resigns in favour of Tupper.

May 1	Tupper sworn in as Prime Minister of Canada.
June 23	Conservatives defeated in the election by Laurier Liberals.
July 2	Governor General refused to allow patronage appointments already granted by the defeated government.
July 8	Government resigns.
July 27	Tupper calls for leadership review; unanimously re-elected leader. Remains leader until 1899.
Oct 8	The Tuppers celebrate 50th wedding anniversary.
1897, Jan 6	Sir Charles retires from the role of High Commissioner to United Kingdom.
1899	Honorary LLD from Queens University.
	Sir Charles and Lady Tupper involved in an accident while crossing the Saskatchewan River at Strathcona in a sleigh.
Nov 6	Defeated in election; retires from public life at age 80.
1901, Jan	Tupper retires from the Conservative leadership.
1901-08	Spends next eight years between England and Canada.
1908	Member of the Privy Council of United Kingdom.
1909	Retires to The Mount in Bexleyheath, outside London.
1912	Frances dies after 66 years of marriage. Tupper accompanies her body to Halifax. Before returning to England visits Hibbert in Vancouver and William in Winnipeg.
1913, Apr	Tupper visits Amherst. Greeted by parade of 2000 people who took a half-holiday to welcome him.
1913-15	In failing health and often visited by Sir William Osler.

1915	Stewart Tupper dies in England from a stroke.
Oct 29	Sir Charles Tupper dies in his sleep.
	The body is returned to Halifax, buried in Fairview Cemetery beside Frances on November 16.
1916	Grandson, Hibbert's son Gordie, killed at the Battle of Vimy Ridge.
1927, Mar 30	Charles Hibbert Tupper (Charlie) dies.
1947	William Tupper dies in Winnipeg.
1967	Sir Charles Tupper Medical Building at Dalhousie University opened as Nova Scotia's centennial project.

The Obituary of Sir Charles Tupper
by Sir William Osler

One of the fathers of Canadian Federation, a distinguished politician, and probably the oldest medical graduate of the University of Edinburgh, Sir Charles Tupper has passed to his rest, full of years and honours, at the patriarchal age of 94. Few men have lived more vigorously, first in the rough and tumble of a large general practice in Nova Scotia and then in a more turbulent area of politics, yet he retained good health of mind and body nearly to the end. Like so many distinguished Nova Scotians, he was of New England stock.

His thesis at Edinburgh was "On the mechanism and management of parturition, illustrated by a report of 116 cases." He was never tired of talking of the happy life spent there as a medical student. Simpson, then newly appointed to the chair of midwifery, was his favourite teacher, and he kept up warm friendships with many of his old professors. Only a few months ago he promised the writer to jot down the reminiscences of his Edinburgh life. Returning to his native town, Amherst, he very quickly had a large and widespread practice. He was fond of surgery, and was one of the few men remaining who could talk of personal experiences in pre-anaesthetic days. He told the writer of an amputation at the hip joint for sarcoma performed on a farmer's wife on the kitchen table, with a sailor as assistant. The patient lived 18 miles away, so he was never able to make a second visit. Three months later the farmer drove to Amherst with his wife strong and well.

At intervals in his busy life he practised his profession at Halifax, Ottawa, and for a year or more at Toronto. He took an active part in the formation of the Canadian Medical Association, and to the end retained keen interest in the progress of medicine.

Canada owes a deep debt to Sir Charles Tupper, and his political opponent, Sir Wilfred Laurier, very truly said that next to Sir John A. MacDonald, the man who did most to being about the federation of the Canadian provinces was Sir Charles Tupper. With a strong and daring personality, he had all the qualities for success in the public life – calmness and clear judgement in victory, resolution and hopefulness in defeat. Nothing in his history was more remarkable than to have "stumped the country" successfully for his party when in his 80th year. A strong imperialist, Sir Charles Tupper once remarked that "the two aims he has always kept in view ...... have been the strengthening of the golden link which connects England with the first and greatest of her colonies and the holding aloft of the standard rite of the nation so that she may prove herself worthy of the proud position she has made her own."

His life is an illustration of the brilliant success of the doctor in politics. We have to go to France or to the South American Republic to parallel his career. But, he never really served two masters; from 1855 he was a politician first, and practitioner only when stranded by the exigencies of party.

A few months ago he, in reply to a question as to what he attributed his kindly old age, said: "a good constitution, a good digestion, and a capacity to sleep." It was in truth his good arteries, which were scarcely palpable when the blood stream was pressed out. Yet here was a man who in 1880 – 1881 was ready to throw out the sponge, as he was believed to have Bright's disease! Some years ago, in a paper "on the advantages of a trace of albumin and a few tube casts in the urine of men above 50 years of age" the writer mentions his case. In 1881 he saw Andrew Clark, who gave most sensible advice, but was inclined to take a gray view of the renal condition. The advantage of the discovery was never better illustrated, as he ever after lived a careful life.

Bibliography

Beck, J. Murray. *The History of Maritime Union: A Study in Frustration*. Fredericton, New Brunswick, 1969. (Maritime Union Study.)

Beck, J. Murray. *The Shaping of Canadian Federalism: Central Authority or Provincial Right?*, Toronto, Copp Clark Publishing Company, 1971, (Issues in Canadian History.)

Beck J Murray. *Joseph Howe: Conservative Reformer. Vol 1, 1804-1848*, Toronto, McGill-Queens University Press, 1982.

Beck, J Murray. *The Government of Nova Scotia*. Toronto, University of Toronto Press, 1957.

Beck J M. *Joseph Howe, Anti-confederate*. Ottawa, Canadian Historical Association, 1965. (Historical Booklet, #17.)

Bruce, Harry. *Here Lies Joseph Howe*. Halifax, The Fourth Estate, 1973.

Berton, Pierre. *The Great Railway*. Toronto: McClelland Stewart Ltd. 1972.

Berton, Pierre. *The Last Spike*. Toronto: McClelland and Stewart Ltd. 1971.

Cameron, Ian. *Halifax and the Cholera Epidemic of 1866*. NS Med Bull 149-153, 1984.

Cameron, James D., *For the People: A History of St. Francis Xavier University*. Montreal and Kingston, McGill-Queen's University Press. 1996. Pages 74-75.

Craggs, R. S. *Sir Adams G. Archibald: Colchester's Father of Confederation*, Truro, NS, Truro News, 1967.

Cushing, Harvey. *The Life of Sir William Osler*. Oxford, Clarendon Press; Vol 2, pp 618-619, 1925.

De Volpi, Charles. *Nova Scotia: A Pictorial Record; Historical Prints and Illustrations of the Province of Nova Scotia, Canada, 1605-1878*. Toronto, Longmans, Canada, 1974.

Dunlop, Allan C. *Vital Statistics in Nova Scotia*. Archivist, Public Archives of Nova Scotia. Unpublished manuscript.

Eaton, Arthur Wentworth Hamilton, M.A., D.C.L. *The History of Kings County Nova Scotia*. The Salem Press Company. Salem, Massachusetts. 1910.

Eyler, J M. *Victorian Social Medicine: The Ideas and Methods of William Farr*. Baltimore, 1979.

Ferguson, C. Bruce. *The Origin of Representative Government in Canada*. Halifax, Committee on Bicentenary of Representative Government, 1958.

Ferguson, C. Bruce. *Joseph Howe of Nova Scotia*. Windsor, NS, Lancelot Press, 1973.

Fingard, Judith. *The Dark Side of Life in Victorian Halifax*. Halifax, Pottersfield Press. 1989.

Foxley, G L. *A History of the Bexleyheath Golf Club, 1907-1977*. Dartford, England, S.B.Printing Co. 1980.

Fraser, W. Hamish and Morris, R.J.. *People and Society in Scotland Volume II, 1830 – 1914*. Edinburgh, John Donald Publishers Ltd.; 1990.

Gibbon, John Murray. *The Victorian Order of Nurses for Canada 50th Anniversary 1897-1947*. Printed by Southam News, Montreal for the Victorian Order of Nurses; 1947.

Grant, A. *The Story of the University of Edinburgh During Its First Three Hundred Years*. 2 vols., London; Longmans, Green & Co., 1884.

Grant, W. L. *The Tribune of Nova Scotia – a Chronicle of Joseph Howe*. Glasgow, Brook & Company; Toronto; 1915.

Hill, K. *The Man Who was Nova Scotia*. Toronto, McClelland and Stewart, 1980.

Heagerty, J. J. *Four Centuries of Medical History in Canada*. Bristol; John Wright & Sons Ltd.; 1928.

Horn, D. B. *A Short History of the University of Edinburgh 1556-1889*, University Press; Edinburgh; 1967.

Howe, Joseph. *Joseph Howe: Voice of Nova Scotia*. A selection, edited and with an introduction by J. Murray Beck. Toronto, McClelland and Stewart, 1964.

Howe, J. *Western and Eastern Rambles: Travel Sketches of Nova Scotia*. Edited by M.G. Parks. Toronto, University of Toronto Press, 1973.

Howell, Colin. *A Century of Care: A History of the Victoria General Hospital in Halifax 1887-1987*. Published by the VGH Foundation. 1988.

Hunt, W.A. (editor), *The Proceedings of the Joseph Howe Symposium*. (Mount Allison University, October 1983); Halifax, Nimbus Publishing Ltd; 1984.

Leacock, Stephen. *Canada: The Foundations of its Future*. Montreal privately printed, by the House of Seagram. 1941.

Longley, J.W. *Sir Charles Tupper*. Toronto. Makers of Canada (Morang) Ltd.; Toronto; 1916; (Parkman Edition).

MacDermot, H.E. *History of the Canadian Medical Association 1867-1921*. Toronto, Murray Printing Company, Limited; 1935.

Marble, Allan E. *Deaths, Burials and Probate of Nova Scotians, 1749-1799*, from Primary Sources. Vol 1 (A-L); Vol 2 (M-Z).

Marble, Allan E. *Surgeons, Smallpox and the Poor*. Montreal, McGill University Press, 1995.

MacDermot, H.E. *History of the Canadian Medical Association 1867-1921*. Toronto, Murray Printing Company, Limited; 1935.

MacEwan, Paul. *Confederation and the Maritimes*. Windsor, NS. Lancelot Press, 1976.

MacIntosh, Alan Wallace. *The Career of Sir Charles Tupper in Canada, 1864-1900*. PhD thesis (unpublished); University of Toronto, 1960. (Killam Library, Halifax copy, F1033T86M25).

McGee, Harold Franklyn. *Atlantic Bibliographies*. St. Mary's University Department of Anthropology. Halifax Steven A. Davis and Michael Taft. 1975.

Meagher, Sir Nicholas H.*The Religious Warfare in Nova Scotia 1855-1860*. (also titled "Howe and the Catholics"), Halifax, privately printed; 1927.

Newman, Lena. *The John A. MacDonald Album*. Montreal Tundra Books of Montreal; 1974.

Osler, Sir William. *The Obituary of Sir Charles Tupper*, Bart. *British Medical Journal*, Nov. 6, 2: 2862; 694-695, 1915; Also in *Lancet* Nov. 6, 2:4810; 1049-1050, 1915, and the *Canadian Medical Journal*, Nov 1915.

Parker, William Frederick. *Daniel MacNeill Parker, MD: His Ancestry and a Memoir of His Life*. Toronto, William Briggs. 1910.

Percy, H. R., *Joseph Howe*. Toronto, Fitzhenry and Whiteside, 1976 (The Canadians).

Pryke, K. G. *Nova Scotia and Confederation, 1864-74*. Toronto, University of Toronto Press, 1979. (Canadian Studies in History and Government).

Rawlyk, G. A. (editor). *Historical Essays on the Atlantic Provinces*. Toronto, McClelland and Stewart. 1967.

Rawlyk, G. A. *Joseph Howe, Opportunist? Man of Vision? Frustrated Politician?* Toronto, Copp Clark, 1967, (Issues in Canadian History).

Ross, George W. *Getting Into Parliament and After*. Toronto: William Briggs, 1913.

Saunders, E.M., D.D. (editor). *The Life and Letters of Rt. Hon. Sir Charles Tupper, Bart., K.C.M.G. Volume I and II.* London, Cassell and Company Ltd. 1916.

Saunders, E.M., D.D. *Three Premiers of Nova Scotia.* Toronto, William Briggs, 1909.

Schull, Joseph. *Laurier: The First Canadian.* Toronto, MacMillan of Canada; 1965.

Shepherd, John A., *Simpson and Syme of Edinburgh.* Edinburgh & London; E. & S. Livingston Ltd.; 1969.

Simpson, J.H.L., *The Life of Sir Charles Tupper. Canadian Medical Association Journal,* June 1939. Also read before the Halifax Medical Society, Halifax NS, February 22, 1939.

Steele, Rev. D.A., and Rogers, G.M., *One Hundred Years With the Baptists of Amherst,* N.S., Amherst, 1911.

Tennant, R.D., *The Quill-and-Rail Catalogue. A Bibliographical guide to Canadian rail roads.* Halifax, Tennant Publishing House, 1976.

Thibault, Charles, *Biography of Sir Charles Tupper.* Montreal. L'Etendard Print. 1883.

Tupper, Rt. Hon. Sir Charles, Bart., G.C.M.G., C.B. *Recollections of Sixty Years.* London, Cassell and Company. 1914.

Tupper, Sir Charles Hibbert. *Supplement to the Life and Letters of the Right Hon. Sir Charles Tupper Bart., K.C.M.G.* Toronto, The Ryerson Press; 1926.

Tupper, E. *Tupper Genealogy: In The Interest of the Tupper Family Association of America.* Beverley, Mass; The Reporter Press; Paul K. Blanchard Inc. North Conway N.H. 03860.

Tupper Papers. Inventory of manuscripts in the Public Archives of Nova Scotia. Halifax 1976.

Vaison, Robert. *Nova Scotia Past and Present; A Bibliography.* Halifax, Nova Scotia, Department of Education, 1976.

Vaison, Robert. *Studying Nova Scotia: Its History and Present State, Its Politics and Economy; A Bibliography and Guide.* Halifax, Mount Saint Vincent University, 1974.

Waite, Peter B. *The Life and Times of Confederation, 1864-1876; Politics, Newspapers and the Union of British North America*. Toronto, University of Toronto Press, 1962.

Waite, Peter B. *The Charlottetown Conference*. Toronto, The Canadian Historical Association, 1970.

Waite, Peter B. *The Man From Halifax: Sir John Thompson, Prime Minister*. Toronto, University of Toronto Press. 1985.

Waite, Peter B. *Macdonald: His Life and World*. Toronto, McGraw-Hill Ryerson, 1975.

Waite, Peter B. *Sir John A. Macdonald: The Man*. Halifax, Dalhousie Review. Summer, 1967, Vol. 47, 1967.

Index

A

Aberdeen, Lady Ishbel, 109, 113, 129

Aberdeen, Governor General Lord, 109, 111, 113

Acadia, 48

Acadia College and University, 15, 49, 53

Alison, William Pulteney, 29, 32, 50

Allan, Sir Hugh, 87

Almon, Emma, 28, 33

Almon, Sophia, 28, 33

Almon, William Bruce, 18, 51, 52

Amherst, 13, 35, 36, 37, 120, 122

Anticonfederation arguments, 66

Anticonfederation movement, 66

Anti-unionist, 68

Archibald, Hon. A.G., 59, 65

Arichat College, 53

Armdale (Tupper's home), 86

Arthur, Captain, 32, 34

Asylum for the Poor, 50, 51

Asylum, Beauport Lunatic, 75

Atlantic Steamship Service, 109

Avery, Dr., 76

B

Bexleyheath, Kent, 114, 120

Bexleyheath, The Manor at, 114, 118

Black, Dr. Rufus, 52

Bordon, R.L., 114, 123

Botheration Scheme, 61

Bowell, Sir Mackenzie, 90, 108, 110, 112

Bowman, Edward (Ned), 27, 32

British Colonist, The, 47

British Commonwealth, 103

British Medical Journal, 122

British North America (BNA) Act, 63, 64, 84, 110

Brown, George, 59, 64

Bulwer-Lytton, Edward, 46

C

Cameron, Captain D.R., 78

Cameron, John, Bishop of Antigonish, 101

Cameron, Emma (Tupper), 38, 78-82

Cameron, Sophie, 86

Campbell, Alexander, 59

Canadian Gazette, 119

Canadian Medical Association, 74-76, 85, 92n., 124

Canadian Medical Association, History of the, 75

Canadian Medical Journal, 75, 122

Canadian Pacific Railroad (CPR), 87-91, 95, 102, 110, 126

Cartier, George Etienne, 59, 69, 71, 87, 99, 106n.

Casgrain, T. Chase, K.C., 123

Charlottetown Conference, 58

Cheadle, Dr. Walter, 70

Cholera, 55-58

Christison, Dr. Robert, 29, 30, 32

Chronology Appendix 1, 133-142

City of York (ship), 70

City Medical Officer, 50

Clarke, Sir Andrew, 96-99, 106n.

Confederation, 58, 70

Connolly, Archbishop, 56

Connelly, Mary Claire, 56

Conservative, 41

Conservative Party, 15

Cowie, Dr. A.J., 52

CPR, *see* Canadian Pacific Railroad

CPR Scandal, 87-89

CPR Syndicate, 101

Cumberland County, 13, 115

Cunard, Samuel, 46

D

DaCosta, Dr., 28

Dalhousie College, 48-50, 76, 77

Dalhousie Medical School, 49, 76-78, 93n., 128

Davies, Dr. W.H., 52

DeWolf(e), Dr. James Ratchford, 23, 27, 33

DeWolfe, Thomas Andrew, 41

Dickey, Hon. Robert, 59

Diphtheria, 50

Doucet, Mary Alphonse, 56

Dufferin, Lord, 87, 88

Durham, Lord, 58

E

Edinburgh, 11, 42, 49

Edinburgh, Royal College of, 32

Edinburgh Royal Infirmary, 26

Edinburgh, University of, 13, 18, 23

Education, free, 52-55

England (steamship), 55

F

Father MacIssac, 56

Father of Confederation, 124

Fathers of Confederation, 58

Fielding, W.S., 102, 118

Fisheries, 68, 85

Fleming, Sir Sandford, 85

Fort Cumberland, 37

Fulton, 41

G

Galt, Alexander, 59, 66, 69, 100

Garvie, Dr. John, 55

Garvie, Dr. Frank, 55

Gordon, Dr. David, 28

Gossip, Dr. Charles, 55

Grant, William Lawson, 43

H

Hamm, Dr. John, 105n.

Hangman's Beach, 55, 56

Harding, Dr. Ebenezer Fitch, 19, 20, 23,

Harding, Reverend Theodore Seth, 19

Hattie, Dr. A., 52

Henderson, Dr. William, 30, 32

Henry, William, 59

Hinds, Dr. Thomas W., 120

Hockney, Pat, 18

Hope, Professor Charles, 25

Horton Academy, 17, 23, 42, 48, 53

Hospital, Minto House, 30

Hospital, Provincial, 50

Howard, Dr. R.P., 96

Howe, Joseph, 38, 41, 42, 43, 47, 48,
50, 59, 60, 65, 66, 67, 69, 70, 71,
76, 82, 86, 99, 126, 129

Huntington (ship), 13, 20

I

Intercontinental Railway, 46, 68, 85, 124

Intercontinental Railway Board, 67, 69

Intercontinental Railway Commission,
65

J

Jameson, Professor Robert, 26

Jennings, Dr. Edward, 52

Jex-Blake, Dr. Sophia, 33

Johnstone, James William, 15, 38, 44

K

Kennedy, Sir Charles, 119

Kings College, 53

Knight Commander of the Order of
St. Michael and St. George
(K.C.M.G.), 86, 102

L

Lancet, 122

Langevin, Hector, 59, 103, 125

Laurier, Wilfred, 104, 108, 116, 122

Lawson, Dr. G., 77

Leacock, Stephen, 38

London Conference, 63

Longley, Avard, 48, 53

Longley, Judge J.W., 36, 53-54

M

Macdonald, John A., 59, 60, 63, 64, 65,
66, 68, 69, 74, 79, 82, 99, 102, 103,
104, 105, 122, 125

Macdonald, Premier John Sanfield, 71

MacFarlane, A., 41

MacKenzie, Alexander, 87, 88

Manitoba schools issue, 109-112

Manor, The Bexleyheath, 118

Maritime Medical News, 85

Marsden, Dr., 75

McKenzie, Mr. Richard J., 25

McCully, Jonathan, 15,16, 53, 59

McDougall, William, 59

McGee, D'Arcy, 59, 64, 68, 71, 99

McGregor, Sister

McNab's Island, 55

Meagher, Sir Nicholas H., 45n.

Medical Faculty, 77

Medical Society of Nova Scotia, 52,
76, 84

Miller, Mr. James, 30, 32

Miller, William, 61

Minister of Inland Revenue, 86

Monck, Lord, 63

Monro, Alexander primus, secundus,
tertius, 24-25

Morning Chronicle, 61, 72

Morning Star, 64

Morse, Alpheus, 37

Morse, Frances Amelia, 37

Morse, Silas Hibbert, 37

Murray, Premier George, 117

N

National Council of Women, 109

National Policy, 85, 89, 95

New York Medical Journal, 96

Normal School at Truro, 53

O

Obituary, Sir Charles Tupper, 143

Onderdonk, Andrew, 91

Osler, Sir William, 96-99, 105n., 118, 120, 121, 122

Ottawa, Canada, 82-83

P

Pacific scandals, 87-89, 94n.

Page, Dr. Benjamin, 16, 17, 23, 36, 38,39

Parker, Dr. Daniel MacNeill, 17, 18, 26, 27, 32, 33, 36, 52, 76, 78, 84, 85, 94n., 102, 105n., 106n., 110

Patronage, 67

Pembina, Northwest Territories, 78, 79, 82

Pictou Academy, 53

Planters, 35

Poor Asylum, 50, 51

Pope, Joseph, 90, 126

Powell, Sir Douglas, 120, 121

Power, Mary Vincent, 56

Prior, Dr. Henry, 52

Pryamus, HMS, 55

Pugsley Pharmacy, 40n., 46

R

Railroad, *see* Canadian Pacific Railway

Reciprocity Treaty, 85

Reid, Dr. A.P., 76, 77

Richot, Father, 80, 81

Riel, Louis, 78-82

Riel, Sister, 80, 93n.

Robertson, Andrew, 102

S

Saint Andrews, New Brunswick, 86, 119

St. Francis Xavier College, 53

St. John's Cemetery, 120, 122

Saunders, E.M., 118

Savage, Dr. John, 105n.

Shannon, S.L., 48

Simpson, Dr. James Young, 26, 31-32

Sisters of Charity, 56

Slayter, Dr. John, 55-58

Slayter, Dr. W.B., 52

Smith, Donald A. 79, 80, 110

Smith, Dr. James, 105n.

Smith, Dr. John, 27, 36

Steamship service, 112

Steele, Dr. John, 105n.

Stewart, Alexander, 37, 38

Stewart, Dr. Chester, 128

Stewart, Emma (Cameron), 38, 121

Stewart, Mary Wilson (Robertson), 128

Stewart, Dr. Ronald, 105n.

Sydney, Cape Breton, 90

Syme, Mr. James, 30

T

Ternan, Dr. John, 52

Thompson, Sir John, 72, 101, 102, 105, 108

Tilley, Leonard, 69, 112

Traill, Professor Thomas Stewart, 26, 32

Tupper, Charles Hibbert, 39, 90, 103, 105, 108, 109, 110, 111, 120, 128

Tupper, Sir Charles, birth, 16; early education, 16-18; family history, 15; genealogy, 21n., Appendix 1, pp 132;

apprenticeship, 19-20;
Edinburgh education, 20-21, 23-33;
country doctor, 35-40;
marriage, 37;
pharmacy, 40n.,
political beginning, 41-45;
comparison with Howe, 42-43;
credo, 47;
medical practice, 35-40, 47;
Dalhousie College, 48-50;
Asylum for Poor, 50-52;
free education, 52-55;
cholera epidemic, 55-58;
Maritime Union, 58-61;
Confederation, 58, 70;
Canadian Medical Association,
74-76, 85, 124;
Dalhousie Medical School, 76-78;
93n., 128;
Ottawa, 82-83;
vital statistics, 83-85;
Pacific Scandals, 87-89, 94n.;
illness, 96-99;
High Commissioner, London, 100-105;
Prime Minister, 112;
Retirement, 114-116;
final illness, 118-121;
obituary, 122-123,
Appendix 2, 143-144;
Chronology, Appendix 1, 133-142.

Tupper, Charlotte, 16

Tupper, Eliakim, 15

Tupper, Elizabeth Stewart, 38-39

Tupper, Emma (Cameron) 38, 78, 114

Tupper, Frances (Morse), 37, 44, 78,79,
86, 88, 102, 109, 113, 114, 116, 119,
121, 122

Tupper, James, 16

Tupper, James Stewart, 39

Tupper, Janet, 110

Tupper, Lily, 120

Tupper, Marie Stewart, 128

Tupper, Martin, 15, 46, 61n.

Tupper, Miriam Lockhart Low(e), 14,
16, 23, 39

Tupper, Dr. Nathan, 16, 22n., 47

Tupper, Nathan, 20

Tupper, Reggie, 121, 124

Tupper, Reverend Charles D.D., 14,
16, 48, 99

Tupper, Sophie, 47, 50, 120

Tupper, Stewart, 120

Tupper, Thomas, 15

Tupper, Captain Victor Gordon, 111,
124n., 124

Tupper, William, 88, 119

Twining, Charles, 52

Tyrell, Mr., 119

U

Uniacke, Richard, 37

United Empire Club, 119

V

Verney, Sir Harry, 69

Victoria, Queen, 28, 46, 65, 108

Victorian Order of Nurses (VON), 109,
113, 116

Virchow, Professor Rudolf, 97, 129

Vital statistics, 83-85

W

Wickwire, Dr. W.N., 50, 55

Williston, John S., 114, 126

Windsor, Nova Scotia, 13, 19

Wolfville, 17, 48

Y

Young, William, 47, 48, 78